CHILDREN AND YOUTH
Social Problems and Social Policy

CHILDREN AND YOUTH
Social Problems and Social Policy

Advisory Editor

ROBERT H. BREMNER

How
Two Hundred Children
Live and Learn

RUDOLPH R. REEDER

ARNO PRESS
A New York Times Company
New York — 1974

Reprint Edition 1974 by Arno Press Inc.

Reprinted from a copy in
  The University of Illinois Library

CHILDREN AND YOUTH
Social Problems and Social Policy
ISBN for complete set: 0-405-05940-X
See last pages of this volume for titles.

Manufactured in the United States of America

Library of Congress Cataloging in Publication Data

Reeder, Rudolph Rex, 1859-
    How two hundred children live and learn.

    (Children and youth: social problems and social
policy)
    Reprint of the 1910 ed. published by Charities
Publication Committee, New York.
    1. Orphans and orphan-asylums--New York (State)--
Hastings on Hudson. I. Title. II. Series.
HV995.H42H47 1974   362.7'32'09747277   74-1701
ISBN 0-405-05978-7

HOW
TWO HUNDRED CHILDREN
LIVE AND LEARN

How
Two Hundred Children
Live and Learn

BY

RUDOLPH R. REEDER, Ph.D.

Superintendent New York Orphan Asylum
Hastings-on-Hudson, New York

NEW YORK
CHARITIES PUBLICATION
COMMITTEE   MCMX

PRESS OF WM. F. FELL CO.
PHILADELPHIA

Table of Contents

List of Illustrations

INTRODUCTION

INTRODUCTION

IN the hotbeds of the Orphanage there are now five thousand tomato plants ready for the market. As you look at them down the long line of garden frames their crimped and frizzled tops present a leafy surface almost as level and velvety as a tapestried floor, and of a deep green color. This fine exhibit of young plants is not the result of accident or empirical effort. The soil in which the seeds were planted was carefully selected, sifted to fineness and mixed with the fertilizer. It was spread in the hothouse frames in three layers, each differing from another in texture and the proportion of fertilizer. The seeds were planted at a certain depth, and the temperature was kept at a fixed degree. Light and moisture were provided in suitable measure to meet the needs of the tiny plantlets. There was such exactness of conditions and such precision of method all along the line as mark scientific procedure. There was no guesswork about it.

Two Hundred Children

A similar description of ways and means would account for the four hundred fluffy little Plymouth Rocks now scratching for a living in the brooder attached to the poultry yard of the Orphanage. But here the product is of a much higher order in the scale of organic development, the functions of individual organs so much more complex and delicate, that still greater care and vigilance were necessary. The successful poultry raiser must be a closer student of the phenomena of natural law and growth than the gardener.

But, besides a garden full of plants and a brooder full of chicks, we have an Orphanage full of children. What shall we say of the possibility of scientific procedure here in this infinitely higher realm of life than that of plant or animal? Did Solomon utter a scientific proposition when he said, "Train up a child in the way he should go and when he is old he will not depart from it"? Is the complexity of structure and function so great in the human species, the personal equation so varied and uncertain in the individual, that it is impossible to formulate the principles of a science of child training? When I spoke to a

Administration Building and Cottages, Hastings-on-Hudson

Introduction

friend a short time ago of the blessings that children bring to a home, he replied, "Yes, children are a great blessing if they turn out well," with an air of uncertainty that might properly characterize his prediction as to the outcome of a game of chance.

Judging from the results one sees in thousands of American homes it would seem as though modern science, which has successfully invaded almost every other realm of human interest, had overlooked that of rearing and training children. How uncertain and haphazard is the whole matter of children's dietary, sleep, play, discipline and household régime!

Those who raise poultry or other live stock give the most careful attention to food and drink. But how capricious and accidental is the dietary of children in a majority of American homes. They eat anything and everything they want with little regulation as to time, quantity or quality. They sleep when nature forces it against the odds of high tension amusements of all sorts, and play without leadership or reference to what is best for the development of mind or body.

Two Hundred Children

It is because of a thoroughly tested and well grounded faith on the part of the author in the efficiency of certain principles and methods of training that this little book is sent forth. It is a record of experience, first with children in rural schools, second with those in a village school, third with those in a city school, fourth with five children of the author's own family, and finally for the past ten years with two hundred children of the New York Orphanage. The little family and the big one—the five and the two hundred—have, of course, furnished the richest field for study and experiment. With these we have lived.

Much of the material herein presented first appeared in a series of fourteen articles in Charities and the Commons—now The Survey—under the title To Country and Cottage. They were written at irregular intervals during 1906, 1907, and 1908, with no attempt at logical arrangement. While each chapter contains considerable new material, chapters eight and nine are almost entirely new.

The writer begs herewith to acknowledge his great indebtedness, as well as to express his deep

First She Loves It, then She Feeds It

Introduction

sense of appreciation, to the Trustees of this
Orphanage for the open-minded, broad-spirited,
large-hearted manner in which they have endorsed
every sane forward movement in his methods
of administration, instruction and training. To
these noble women and to another, whose inspiration, ready suggestion and sympathetic interest at
all times have brought her into spiritual joint
authorship, my wife, this little volume is affec-
tionately dedicated.

I
DIETARY, FOOD INTERESTS AND INCENTIVES

I

THE first act of the new-born child is to breathe; the second, to exercise his body, and the third, to eat. Fresh air to breathe, range and freedom of exercise, and plenty of wholesome food for the growing body are the conditions for physical well-being. Food is the fuel that supplies the energy for exercise and growth.

"Man is what he eats and what he does with it." If this proposition savors too much of the animal to be entirely true of adult human beings, it is certainly not far from the truth when applied to growing children. Food and clothing go along with air and exercise as first requisites of the new-born child. They continue to be of the first importance throughout childhood.

Any need that is easily observed and apparent to every one is pretty sure to be well looked after in children's institutions. This is true of clothing. Almost any casual observer can tell whether the children are decently and comfortably clothed;

Two Hundred Children

hence, children in institutions are usually comfortably although not often tastefully dressed. To skimp and save beyond the point of comfort or decency would at least expose the administration to criticism.

But in an institution of two hundred children it would be an easy matter to reduce the per capita allowance of food, or to change to inferior brands of food stuffs for a week, month or longer period of time, and thereby save a considerable sum without any one knowing it except the mute, innocent victims of such vicious economy. Even the children may not know that their food is insufficient. There is a difference between filling and food, but the child may not be conscious of it—some older people are not—even though the physical condition betrays it to the careful observer. Failure to provide a nutritious dietary in sufficient quantity and variety is, I believe, one of the most common defects of institutional administration, even in these days of plenty and in this land "flowing with milk and honey."

Not long ago I visited an institution for orphan children, arriving just at the supper hour. When

Dietary and Food Interests

near the dining room I noticed a strong odor of tea, and soon learned that the children's supper consisted of tea, crackers and cheese. I marveled at such a menu for children, and wondered in what quantities castor oil was supplied to the institution.

The child is the victim, first, of the grocer and butcher, who wish the institution trade and are obliged to secure it by competitive bids. This system has developed institutional grades of various food stuffs—beans that are rusty, wormy and unsorted; molasses that will tarnish a silver spoon; stale oatmeal poorly screened and infested with weevil; tea that reminds one of musty hay, and prunes with a thin skin stretched over large pits.

All of this may do for filling, but it is not good food.

Second, the child is the victim of indifferent and easy-going cooks and their helpers, who think almost any sort of attention and preparation will do for a "lot of children." Little effort is made to make the food really palatable and attractive, well seasoned or tempting to the appetite. Where the cooking is done on a large scale, the food stuffs are handled like stock feed, shoveled in and scooped out. Quantity, not quality, is the matter of chief concern. Not long ago our cooking teacher was informed that the children in one of our cottages did not like hash. When the next cooking lesson was given in that cottage the efforts of the class were concentrated on making good hash. The meat was chopped fine, gristle and bone removed, onions, potatoes and gravy carefully proportioned to the amount of meat, and the whole brought to a rich, tempting brown, seasoned to taste and served hot, with an odor that was irresistible. It is needless to say that all of the children liked hash at that supper.

Such an object lesson from time to time tones up the institution cooking as well as the tastes of the children, whose naturally keen appetites make them uncritical. Since children complain less than older people about the quality of their food, children's cooks are pretty sure to concern themselves chiefly with the quantity required, and therefore select menus that need but little preparation for the table. Plenty of liquids, like

Dietary and Food Interests

milk, tea, coffee; cereals hurriedly and carelessly prepared; bread from the bakery, etc.—such a dietary gives the cook an easy time of it. The child soon becomes accustomed to having everything that he eats soft, and really prefers it to more solid food, which would be much better for him. His bread is always dipped into milk, tea or coffee; he chews but little. His teeth decay early from lack of use, and there is less than the normal flow of the digestive fluids. Eating is simply filling up. The result is an ill nourished, pasty looking, under-sized child.

In his book "The Bitter Cry of the Children," Mr. John Spargo calls attention to the fact that children who have only bread and coffee for breakfast, and bread and tea for supper, must be patiently taught to eat wholesome food. They have become so accustomed to such unnutritious diet that proper food such as eggs and milk does not attract them. "They are weak and unhealthy as the result of chronic underfeeding." We have received children into this Orphanage who brought with them a developed taste and morbid craving for tea, and who had to learn to drink milk.

Two Hundred Children

I have before me the published weekly menu for one of our large orphanages, in which coffee is served regularly for breakfast. In another institution for children, coffee, tea or cocoa occur frequently in the suppers. Whatever may be claimed in favor of tea and coffee as beverages for adult constitutions, it is certain that they are not food for children. What the child needs is food rather than stimulant. Tea and coffee may stimulate or fill up, but they do not nourish. To substitute either of them for milk is like serving extremely thin soup for a good stew. Why they should be prescribed at all in children's dietaries I have never been able to understand, unless simply to follow the tendency in institutions to reduce the dietary to the lowest terms of economy in money and labor. The result in such cases is also pretty sure to be the lowest terms in food values and nutritive energy.

It is important to provide for children a well balanced dietary. In the published weekly menu of an institution for babies, "baked potatoes" appears every day in the week, while rice and cornstarch each appears twice. Such a dietary certainly lacks suit-

Dietary and Food Interests

able balance and proportion. By referring to the pamphlet "Dietaries for Charitable Institutions," by Miss Florence R. Corbett, issued by the State Board of Charities, which is a most helpful discussion of this question, it may readily be seen that potatoes, rice and cornstarch rank high in the same food element, namely, carbo-hydrates, and thus the menu is very one-sided. By a judicious use of such a schedule of food values as the above report contains, the steward of any institution or family can easily select menus containing the proper proportions of food elements and at the same time provide a pleasing variety of food materials. The smaller the group of children, the easier it is to cater to their needs and tastes. Here the cottage plan of housing offers great advantages over the congregate system.

It is not simply adequate nourishment and a good proportion of nutrients but a variety of food stuffs that is needed. The besetting sin of institution menus is their monotony. When formally made out by a committee, and published, they move steadily on through the year unaffected by seedtime or harvest, the market or changes of the seasons. Sweet potatoes may be cheaper than white tubers, as they frequently are for a month or two each year, but the cut-and-dried institution menu cannot take advantage of this change in price. So it is with fresh fruit and vegetables. At certain times they may be cheaper than the regularly prescribed article, and be both food and medicine for the child; but a fixed menu will not admit of market or seasonal adjustment.

Another unfortunate feature of the prescribed daily menu is the mere fact that the child soon learns it by heart and thus knows beforehand just what he is going to have and how it will be served. At this moment of writing the pleasantest thought I have about my lunch for today is that I don't know what it will be.

"After they had tucked themselves in bed a voice very near me, and which I recognized as Julia's, whispered:

"'May, are yez asleep?'

"'No,' muttered May.

"'Say, is to-morrow bean or molasses day?'

One of Our Cottage Homes

Dietary and Food Interests

"'Bean,' replied May: and then all was silent in the dormitory."*

It would be an insuperable task to make pancakes, gems or rolls for two or three hundred children, but when these are divided up into groups of twenty or twenty-five in separate cottages, each with its own kitchen, the task comes within the limits of an ordinary undertaking.

Soon after the children of this Orphanage had settled in their new cottage homes, the boys of one of the cottages begged the cook to make pancakes for breakfast. When she protested that making pancakes for twenty-five boys was beyond her capacity, they gladly took upon themselves the responsibility, and a great feast of pancakes was spread the next morning. That was but the beginning of innumerable forms of catering to their taste now going on every day in the various cottages. Enough children in each cottage are taking part in the preparation of the meals of the cottage to bring the whole group close to the daily food supply and to give them a voice in it. A few

* Richardson, "The Long Day," page 178.

27

days ago when eggs were issued to one of the cottages on the basis of two to each child, the children decided to eat but one apiece for the first meal and to put the other twenty-five together to be scrambled. At another time, by a similar agreement, they contributed one egg apiece for an omelet.

A lesson in cooking is given every week to the girls of each cottage. It usually begins with a quiz on what may be done with the left-overs from previous meals stored in the refrigerator. In this manner the economy of household science becomes a necessary and practical feature of each lesson. It is a simple matter for a good cook to prepare a meal with all new materials, but to dovetail a few new things into the old in such a way as to give the old new relish and flavor is both a science and an art. Thousands of homes are made unhappy or entirely broken up, while delicatessen stores increase and flourish, just for the want of such skill and economy on the part of wives and mothers.

When the question of the best use of the left-overs has been settled, the new supplies needed are deter-

Dietary and Food Interests

mined, and the lesson rounds up in a regular meal for the whole cottage family. It is, therefore, never just a cooking lesson, taught in a room that is not a kitchen but only a schoolroom. Before another lesson is given a week later, the members of the class must prepare and serve at least two meals in their cottage, embodying the special features of the previous lesson.

Notwithstanding the fact that an all-round training in cooking is given each girl, special aptitudes and tastes develop. Thus, Emily has a reputation for making excellent rolls, Laura for her splendid salads, Marian for popovers that melt in your mouth, Hortense for her graham gems, Frieda for the best layer-cake on the place, etc. These various gifts and tastes introduce the elements of surprise, expectation and variety into the cottage menu. Every time a girl is given an opportunity to apply her skill and taste in one of these directions, the cottage receives the benefit of it.

There is perhaps no better practical test of an institution dietary than a carefully kept record of the growth of the children. It is a simple matter

Two Hundred Children

to balance the scale beam and at the same time read the height of each child on a graduated bar as he stands on the scales. It doesn't cost much to get the scales, and with the standard tables of weights and heights at various ages before you, it may readily be determined whether the children of an institution are above or below average, and to what extent; also whether they are making satisfactory growth from year to year. By applying the above tests the following records for seven years ending November, 1906, were made upon the children of this institution:

Date	No. of Children Weighed and Measured	No. above Standard Average in both Weight and Height	No. below Standard Average in both Weight and Height
1900	161	39	87
1901	166	52	66
1902	177	67	67
1903	165	66	62
1904	174	80	49
1905	174	78	54
1906	171	72	55

The number wanting to make the total in each of the above cases includes all those crossed in various ways with the standard averages, such

Dietary and Food Interests

as those above in height and below in weight, and vice versa. Children under six years are not included, as our standard table does not give averages for these.

Immediately after the first of the above records was taken, various changes in dietary were introduced with a view to bringing up to average as many as possible of those who were below. Among these changes and additions were the following: Graham flour from which brown bread, muffins and gems were made for breakfast or supper; cracked wheat occasionally in place of oatmeal; hasty pudding of cornmeal with molasses for winter suppers; whole wheat flour pudding with raisins served with milk; brown sugar with bread and milk for supper. In addition to the common white beans, the dried red kidney and lima beans were given as a variety; also dried peas. These are not expensive like canned peas, but furnish a pleasing variety. The mere difference in color sometimes adds relish. Lemons three times a month throughout the year provide a much needed food element. A limited amount of dried fruit including apricots, plums, pears, and pitted cherries, for an occasional meal, especially in the latter part of winter, are very wholesome. In the fall and early winter when apples are cheap, apple sauce is a frequent dessert. Salt salmon or mackerel as a change from codfish does not add much to the expense, while providing a pleasant change. Salt salmon cooked soft and mixed with mashed potatoes furnishes a good variety. In winter, a good, hot, vegetable soup for supper containing plenty of tomatoes and onions or carrots, with a little celery, and baked beans with hot brown bread for breakfast, give energetic and healthy tone to growing children. An attractive dessert makes an excellent finish for children's dinners. It is something to look forward to during the first courses of the meal. In addition to rice and tapioca, steamed puddings containing a few apples or apricots, served with milk, and in the apple season, apple dumplings, are economic but relishable desserts.

There is another and very interesting point of view from which to look at the matter of food and dietary in their relation to children. Almost every instinctive interest of the child not only

Our Garden School. Eighty Individual Gardens

Dietary and Food Interests

ministers to the natural wants of the animal life, but may take on also an upward sweep in which the higher concerns of the individual and of society are involved. Thus, the appetite as an incentive may serve a cultural as well as a physiological need. The oldtime schoolmaster had to "treat" the school at Christmastide, or be locked out of the schoolhouse and afterward travel a thorny road with his obstreperous pupils for the rest of the term. On visiting day at the Orphanage this gastronomic incentive is uppermost with the younger children, and under its stimulus they will dispatch the morning tasks with promptness and thoroughness in order to meet their friends with a hearty welcome in the afternoon as they climb the hill with a basket or box under the arm. The greeting is certain to be more enthusiastic if the box is in evidence. Once each month we are reminded of that interesting old story in the school readers of twenty-five years ago—"The Three Boys and the Three Cakes." There are stingy Peters and generous Harrys in every group of children. Many a swap and dicker, cross-your-heart promise and exchange of good-fellowship has been entered into during the month on the speculative strength of what next visiting day will bring forth.

Often on Saturday afternoons, however, there is a crate of oranges, or a barrel of apples or bananas on sale at wholesale rates at the Orphanage supply store, and if the visiting relative has forgotten to bring the box he has surely not left his purse at home. A short walk about the grounds will conveniently round up at the Orphanage fruit counter, where the boy who does business on a commission basis will be anxious to serve all visiting friends and relatives.

The fact that such an opportunity to buy fruit and sweetmeats is offered every week or two, stimulates a good deal of wage-earning industry among the children, and fills many an otherwise idle hour with useful employment. The desires of the appetite thus become a great aid to discipline and self control. The child has something to do and something to work for. One of the great evils of institution life is lack of motivation or incentives. Much of the child's time both in school and out of it is empty and dreary mo-

Dietary and Food Interests

notony. Young life needs nothing so much as proper incentive, and while the motive that fills up waste hours with labor for the purchase of a feast which is soon over, is not of high rank, it is far preferable to fear, enforced restraint or surveillance, which must function when industrial employment is not provided for idle hours.

Ice cream sodas, love of gingerbread, and other appetite incentives may be used in a very effective and wholesome manner when properly correlated with other interests and activities necessary to the development of the child. In fact, a child's life is barren without them. It is too much to ask that the little child shall simply eat to live. Eating *is* living with the healthy, normal, growing child. In this respect it is like playing. And as in the kindergarten we turn play into preparation for life by directing the voluntary and unconscious instincts of the child, so may we use the pleasures of the appetite in a similarly delightful and yet educative manner.

It would be difficult to estimate the value of the appetite incentives in the training of the boys and girls of this Orphanage. In the old home, on the congregate plan, with its large central kitchen, huge range, steam cookers and heavy utensils, there was but little opportunity for the children to assist in any manner connected with the preparation and serving of the regular meals. They marched to the dining room for their three plain, simple meals each day. Of course, there were occasional red-letter days, when turkey, fruit and confectionery brightened up the somber hues of the old dining room. Outside of these special days, however, there was but little variety. There couldn't be very much where courses must be provided on such a large scale by the same cook from day to day, and where no individual tastes were consulted. Under such conditions, the child soon learns the regular order of the limited menu, and as he marches in line into the dining room can predict with certainty what he will see on the table. Eating satisfies the demands of physical growth and waste only. There is little delight and no exhilaration in it. Add to this a severe plainness and sameness of table furnishing, with no tablecloths, no napkins but the blouse sleeve, and with absolute silence thrown in, (as an institution

Dietary and Food Interests

employee once said to me, "Our discipline is fine! Why in our dining room you can hear a pin drop"), and you have all the necessary conditions for the child to eat to live.

Just to live! Think for a moment how large a part of one's pleasures in life, yours and mine, arises from anticipations and surprises concerning the make-up and variety of our daily menus, refinements of the culinary art, chafing-dish skill, etc.; and then consider how much keener is a child's appetite and how much more important in his estimation are all of the interests relating to it, and you will have some conception of the strength of the appetite incentives in children.

A visitor to one of our cottages some time ago found two boys sitting by the kitchen range watching the biscuit. The kitten was drowsing on a chair between them. One of the boys opened the oven door and with the pride of a young chef said, "Let me show you our biscuit; this pan is for Mrs. A. (the cottage matron), and these two are for the boys; we made them ourselves. It's the cook's day off."

Go into a cottage on the morning of July Fourth.

Two Hundred Children

Here are three girls in the kitchen, one baking bread, one making cherry pies with cherries gathered early in the morning by the younger children, and one preparing vegetables. In the pantry two girls are polishing the silverware, in the dining room two are arranging some flowers from their own flower beds. But the center of interest is in the basement, where four girls are making the ice cream. One is cracking the ice with an old axe, one is putting in the salt and two are turning the freezer. A saucer and spoon are close at hand to sample the mixture. What flavor? Chocolate; it was decided upon by vote this morning at the breakfast table. No ice-cream wagons drive in here; we make it ourselves and we have it pretty often in hot weather.

These are but typical and illustrative incidents which occur daily where children and the kitchen live close together, and home industries are made a part of child training. In this Orphanage of two hundred children, not less than sixty are in daily or weekly touch and training with kitchen industries.

This close individual connection with one of the

Dietary and Food Interests

central home interests has a wider social significance than we may at first realize. Space here
will not permit us to discuss this point, but the
following statement from Robert Hunter's book,
"Poverty," bears upon it: "By far the largest
part, eighty per cent at least, of crimes against
property and against the person are perpetrated
by individuals who have either lost connection
with home life, or never had any, or whose homes
have ceased to be sufficiently separate, decent and
desirable to afford what are regarded as ordinary
wholesome influences of home and family."

To say that boys will have little or no use in
after life for such training as we have above
described is no valid argument against it. In
this age of highly specialized forms of adult
occupation, the same objection could be raised
against a score of other attainments, some of
which we think it important to teach to children in our schools. Are we not all of us,
three times a day all our lives, "up against" the
question of how best to prepare, cook and serve
our daily meals? And do we not daily sit in
judgment on the manner in which it is done for

us? Is it not both educative and practical to
have an intelligent comprehension of this most
home-centered of all common industries? There is
little danger that we shall make a mistake in our
curriculum, or miss the mark, either educationally
or practically, so long as we keep within the limits
of the fundamental occupations of life. The tramp
army is not recruited from the ranks of those who
have been well trained in the home-making industries.

But the cottage kitchen is more than simply a
training school for the boys and girls who learn
to prepare the daily meals in it. In the development of a home feeling and home attachment, the
kitchen counts for more than any other feature of
orphanage life. Every man or woman reared in
the earlier homes of this country and in some of
the homes of today, will retain through all suc-
ceeding years sweet memories of the dear old
kitchen. How we looked forward to dinner or
supper when a course of special interest to us was
to be served! The first peas and green corn of
the season, which we helped to gather and prepare
for the cooking; the apple dumplings, pumpkin

Dietary and Food Interests

pies, doughnuts and gingerbread, in the preparation of which we had some share, even though it was but to make the fire, have never tasted since as they did when we smelled them in the old kitchen and looked forward to a feast, with appetites which needed no sauce but opportunity.

The children in the cottages of this Orphanage begin to enjoy the Thanksgiving dinner by nine o'clock in the morning, from which time there is a continuous feast of savor, flavor, or both, until after the one o'clock dinner is served.

A restaurant dinner served from a central kitchen may do for business men and busy women, but the early home of childhood is seriously incomplete without the kindling wood and kitchen stove, the singing kettle and the odor of the boiling pot, the pantry and the cooky jar. If the movement from congregate to cottage system has for its ideal the typical home, the imitation should be made as complete in every respect as possible. To leave the kitchen and dining room, or either of them, out of the cottage home is to attempt the play of Hamlet with the Prince of Denmark left out.

Two Hundred Children

The appetite incentive may be made to function in a very helpful way in correlation with a number of other industries outside the cottage. Our children's garden enterprise is an example of a closely related interest. The child waters, weeds and cultivates his radish, lettuce and onion beds day after day in order that he may have fresh vegetables of his own to eat, sell or give to his friends. If he thinks the price we offer for his radishes too low he eats them himself. There were so few radishes offered to the Orphanage by the children last week that we raised the price. There was a stir in the vegetable market at once, and many an honest penny jingled in the pockets that had previously been carrying radishes for handy lunches while on the playground. Those who had consumed or given away all their crop regretted their inability to share in the advance in price. The pleasure to a child of turning part of his crop into cash and then investing a part of his cash in candy, oranges or ice cream soda, is a wholesome triumph of the appetite incentive. Such radishes are good without salt, and the candy they buy is the sweetest made. Estimate the value of such

Dietary and Food Interests

experiences to children, if you can. It is life, not a cold-storage preparation for life.

Again, the appetite incentive functions in a helpful way in the cooking classes. The interest in each new recipe is not wholly scientific, for the members of the class always liberally sample the product of their own skill and share in the meal which the lesson prepares.

Our ancestors, both English and German, made use of the appetite incentive to teach their children to read, as we learn from the poet, Matthew Prior, and from the great leader of the Philanthropinum, Bernard Basedow. Prior says:

> "To master John the English maid
> A horn-book gives of ginger bread;
> And that the child may learn the better
> As he can name, he eats the letter.
> Proceeding thus with vast delight
> He spells and gnaws from left to right."

Basedow said: "The children must have breakfast, and it is not necessary for any child to eat the alphabet more than three weeks. The cost of shaping the dough into letters is less than a half-penny daily for each child. This makes three

Two Hundred Children

pence a week, or for four weeks, einen groschen. The acquisition is surely worth so much, and it is possible even to the poor children. In each large city there should be ein eigener schulbacker.''

"The bakers to increase their trade
Made alphabets of gingerbread,
That folks might swallow what they read;
All the letters were digested,
Hateful ignorance detested."

II

EXERCISE, ENVIRONMENT AND PLAY

II

NEXT in importance to a well selected and well balanced dietary for the growing child are exercise and environment. In infancy he should not be bandaged, laced up or done up in frills in such a manner as to interfere with frequent stretching and the free use of his body and limbs. In childhood it is not necessary that he should have a gymnasium, but free exercise in a plastic environment that challenges his energy and strength at every turn will answer every necessary purpose.

Unfortunately, the vast majority of children in institutions pass their days amid surroundings that are dull, stale and unresponsive. The child delights in material that he can change and shape at will. He will amuse himself by the hour upon a sand pile or with a lump of putty, a handful of dough or anything that he can shape to the suggestions of his fancy. Herein lies the chief charm in mud pies and rag dolls. Almost "any old thing" that the child can handle with ease and immunity is more entertaining and instructive than that which is fixed, inflexible or easily soiled.

There is but little that the child can do with asphalt pavement, brick walls, iron railings or stone steps. These confront him at every turn in the city home. He is himself in the plastic and formative period of growth and needs for his development a plastic environment. He will learn much through his fingers and toes if they are allowed to come into contact with earth, air, sunshine, water, and animated nature. Brick, stone and asphalt undergo but slight changes with the march of the seasons. Winter and summer with them differ in temperature only. Such solid, non-plastic forms were never intended to surround the home of childhood. Year after year during the early period of child life spent within the narrow confines of an institution so unchangeably and inflexibly environed, can but stupefy the senses and arrest spiritual development. The best place for a child to perform the natural function of change and growth is in an environment that changes and grows. Nature alone can furnish this.

Environment and Play

The miracle of the changing seasons, the myriad forms of life that burst into being with the first days of spring, the opening buds, the first notes of the songsters among the trees, the plowing and planting, the gorgeous glow of sunrise, and the varied tints of sunset—all these teach lessons that are not found in books nor imparted by words. Let the child run and skip in Nature's own laboratory. To go barefoot in the cool, soft grass and mellow ploughed field; to wade in the plashy pool; to smell the newmown hay and the honeysuckle; to look on orchards blossoming; to find rabbits' and birds' and squirrels' nests; to observe the changes that come over cloud and air and sky from the "dewy freshness of early dawn to the restful calm of evening"; to sit in the shade of trees; to swing upon the pendant branches; to catch fireflies; to swim, to skate, to look up at the stars; to watch the gathering storm; to recognize God's power in lightning and thunder, in torrent and gale; to walk to church along a country road; to gather wild flowers as you go; to search for apples in the orchard grass, or chestnuts in the woods; to pick cherries from topmost branches with cherry-stained lips and fingers; to prepare the garden soil; to plant seeds and watch them grow, to cultivate flowers; to feel a part of all one sees and hears and does—this is life and this is childhood.

> "Oh for boyhood's time in June,
> Crowding years in one brief moon,
> When all things I heard or saw,
> Me, their master, waited for.
> I was rich in flowers and trees,
> Hummingbirds and honey bees;
> For my sport the squirrel played,
> Plied the snouted mole his spade;
> For my taste the blackberry cone
> Purpled over hedge and stone;
> Laughed the brook for my delight
> Through the day and through the night."

This free communion with Nature is real soul nourishment and soul expansion. It furnishes the intellect with a wealth of fundamental ideas first hand; it quickens and exalts the imagination, stores the memory with "fair and noble forms and images" which will abide through all the ordeals with books and pedagogues, with business or professional reverses, with whatever awaits us of good or evil report.

READY TO COAST THE LONG HILL

DOING STUNTS ON THE BARS

Environment and Play

In all this I have but imperfectly described the outdoor life and opportunities of the boys and girls of the New York Orphanage. In such an environment there is nothing hard, inflexible and unchanging. Earth and air and sky furnish the raw material of education, and the child is in constant touch with the plastic and shapable. The range and wealth of ideas, as well as the value of the experience that arises out of such contact, is inestimable. Cities are not built with regard for the wants and requirements of childhood. To take the children of this Orphanage back to their city home after a year of rural life here would be almost imprisonment for them. And yet their old home in the city included an entire block with much more spacious and beautifully located grounds than those of most institutions within the city limits.

But a rural environment reacts in other ways than those already mentioned. A child so surrounded, and stimulated by the elixir of pure air and Nature's sweetness and beauty, becomes more active, more dynamic than the child that is in contact with the fixed and the monotonous. He will grow faster, kick out more pairs of shoes, wear out more clothes, eat more, meet with more accidents requiring minor surgery, and probably get into more mischief than his less strenuous brother. But his mischief is also more natural and wholesome, more open and aboveboard, more the outburst of an exuberant spirit than the deliberate planning of an over-restrained child.

When children are cramped for play space, as thousands in the city are, they are obliged to steal much of their fun. They are forbidden here and not allowed there and prohibited in some other direction until they are forced by the irresistible play instinct within to scheme and plan all sorts of covert methods to find amusement for themselves. They become as expert in dodging policemen or caretakers or shopkeepers as in escaping cars and trucks. They play "hide and seek" with the officers of the law, and thus start out in life headed in the wrong direction—against, instead of for, the safeguards of society. What a pity for a child that is by nature social and good-willed, to be forced by circumstances to become unsocial and sullen from the very beginning.

Environment and Play

Give the child plenty of room and plenty of workable material and all this is changed. But this means that the crowded street, the shopkeeper, the caretaker and the man in blue coat and brass buttons should all be left behind, and the fields and woods, the trees and brooks, wild flowers and fruits, substituted for them.

Within the grounds of this Orphanage there are over one hundred cherry trees, every one of which has been "shinned up" many times by the boys, and most of them by the girls. Half as many apple trees have contributed in a similar manner to the children's dietary and athletics. The chestnut trees are so numerous that they have not been counted, but the leaves and grass of every square foot under them have been raked over again and again by little hands and feet with each recurring autumn. A pocketful of nuts gathered one at a time in this way is worth a bushel bought in the market. It is like a string of fish that you have caught with your own hook.

The brook and the river, and where they meet—the swimming beach, have furnished pleasures and triumphs that will live as long as memory lasts.

Two Hundred Children

Fifty-eight boys and girls learned to swim during the summer just past.

All this and much more than is above enumerated is what we mean by an environment that is plastic. It means a succession of interests and opportunities all the year around. Each season brings a whole troop of new things. And Nature never tells the same old story in the same old way; there are always enough surprises in it to keep the child awake and alert. Would that every child might sit close to Nature's heart and hear the story for himself.

> "Then Nature, the old nurse,
>   Took the child upon her knee,
>   Saying, 'Here is a story book
>   Thy Father has written for thee.' "

One of the old school readers of a half century ago contained the following:

> "With books or work or healthful play
>   Let your first years be passed:
>   That you may give for every day
>   Some good account at last."

In our modern improved methods of sifting out economic values from what was formerly waste material, we have not to any great extent redeemed the time of early childhood. In fact, we hardly think of the period of childlife as being so well planned as "to give for every day some good account," or any account at all.

The problem of the parent and the teacher is to bring about such a proper adjustment of the three factors of the above formula—play, work and school—as will leave no room for waste time. Usually we think of waste time as more closely related to play than to work, and yet it is possible to waste time in work quite as easily as in play. Too much work, or work not adapted to the child, will waste his time as seriously as too much play, or play that is empty and without creative interest.

It is as natural, necessary and beautiful for children to play as for kittens to frolic or minnows to swim. But even in these days of "child study" and kindergartens, the importance of developing this instinct of children has not yet been generally recognized by parents and teachers. Less than a generation ago it was a school offence for a child to amuse himself by drawing pictures, and even now parents, and also teachers, except kindergartners

Two Hundred Children

and play directors, who take more than a mere passive interest in the plays of children, are not numerous. When visitors to the Orphanage find me working at the desk they frequently offer an apology for taking my time, but such courtesy seems to them unnecessary if they find me on the playground with the boys and girls. That is "only play." In my judgment, however, it is as important as any work that I can do, even to the conducting of devotional exercises.

In the training of children anywhere, whether in home, school or institution, the degree of individual freedom that may be permitted, or of individual attention given, is in inverse ratio to the number cared for. It is a case in which mere increase of quantity necessarily produces a change in quality. Two or three curious pedestrians may stop when or where they please along the street, but if two or three hundred should avail themselves of such a privilege at the same time and place, they would be ordered to "move on." One or two boys may ascend or descend the stairway by leaps and bounds, but if a hundred or even fifty boys should attempt such freedom of loco-

The Old Home in the City. Erected in 1836

motion the result would be appalling to all who haven't strong nerves; and we would call it disorder.

So it happens that where large numbers of children are cared for in one place, system and order regulate and control many of the ordinary activities of childhood. The program for every day is definitely planned, the child's life is under constant surveillance—or coercion—and but little opportunity is given for initiative or natural reaction. In most institutions the system is so precise and mechanical, the daily routine so simple, and the spatial boundaries are so contracted, that a roll-call might be taken at any hour of the twenty-four and all heads be accounted for.

Under such conditions there is little or no opportunity for the natural feelings or motives of the children to express themselves; all is artificial and conventional, not to say forced. Even the play hour is a period of restraint,—if not made so by teachers or caretakers, it at least becomes so by the mass of children and the narrow quarters allotted for play space. No two or three or small group of children can control for their pleasure any little game or play without molestation from others not in harmony with the sport. The result is that only the simplest, emptiest plays, such as sliding down a board or rolling a hoop, are indulged in. When toys or play apparatus adapted to a higher order of play are presented to children thus situated, the play value cannot be realized for want of opportunity, and the toys are usually quickly disposed of because of the loose tenure of property rights.

One of the earliest and most cherished interests of the child, is possession; and one of the first words he learns to say, is "mine." But in institution life these rights and interests are rudely trampled upon by the dead levelism of the mass. It would not be so bad if this tyrannical evener of individual qualities dominated the study or work hours only, and the child were left free to express his natural self in play, as is the case with the child of the public school.

But institution life need not be so barren, and ought not to be. Much of the child's lost heritage can be restored to him, and no doubt will be when the modern play renaissance, upon which we

Environment and Play

are just entering, gives to this interest of child life its proper place.

Play is the first form or stage of most of the serious purposes of later life. The beginnings of language, literature, art, domestic and scientific interest, common industries, etc., are all play forms. They are the foundation and foreground, the true microcosm of adult experience. Other foundation can no man lay than is laid in the nature of the child. To ignore it, or fail to build upon it, will surely arrest the development of the child and stupefy his mental faculties. The first requisite of play is a maximum of freedom for the child with a minimum of interference on the part of older people.

The importance of freedom, spontaneity and richness in the play life of the child can scarcely be overestimated. Jean Paul says, "I am afraid of every hairy hand and fist that paws in among this tender pollen of child flowers, shaking off here one color, there another, so as to produce just the right carnation." But this is just what we do when we mass under one roof hundreds of children, and then provide through system or organization

59

a routine of activities for almost every hour of the day. Play is Nature's kindergarten and preparatory school of life. The kitten chases its tail, the puppy tears its master's slipper, and the little lamb skips in the meadow that all of them may grow, enjoy life, and become better prepared for making a living and for self-preservation in adult existence.

The most important thing for a little child to do is to grow, and the next most important thing for him to do is to play. But these two are very closely related. There cannot be healthy growth of both mind and body without healthful play.

It is a well-known fact that children pass through successive stages of play development. Young children from four to eight years of age enjoy plays that are highly imaginative. Their delight is to rear most imposing and fanciful superstructures upon very slight foundations of material and fact. The dramatic and make-believe qualities are largely in evidence. These fancy flights are the purest spiritual activity, the very poetry of childhood. To condition or environ the child so as to inhibit this free expression of the imagination is

Environment and Play

to clip the wings of a bird just learning to fly, and thus arrest a natural development.

Rich, interesting, educative play usually requires material, and costs something. But if play is as necessary as industrial occupation, or school, in early life, it is just as important for the child to succeed in his play enterprises as in his more serious undertakings. Successful play will set up aims and through patience and struggle realize them. It will issue in a feeling of triumph. Four of our boys have today built a snow fort with tunnel retreats and towering flagstaff. They have worked hard at it and triumphantly accomplished what they set out to do. Other groups of boys are making similar warlike preparations, stimulated by the blizzard snowfall and the great war in the east. That the very atmosphere on top of the Orphanage hill will be charged with militant zeal no one doubts who knows boy nature.

Sometimes all the child needs in order to succeed in his play ventures is encouragement or suggestion. Sometimes it is raw material and sometimes money. Whatever form of assistance is necessary to successful play should be provided, just as textbooks and apparatus are furnished for his school work.

The child that is constantly disappointed in his play enterprises, making a failure of his cherished play dreams day after day, receiving no sympathy from those responsible for his welfare and no help in overcoming obstacles too great for him, soon loses confidence in himself, falls into the habit of making a failure of what he undertakes, and thus prepares the way for abortive efforts in the more serious ventures of later life. On the other hand, the boy who succeeds in building snow forts, in making his own sled, in coasting the long hill, in hitting the mark with a snowball, in skating, in swimming, in climbing trees, in football, in baseball, in playing marbles; and the girl that dresses her own dolls, builds her own playhouse, coasts the long hill with her own "flexible flyer," provokes to a snow fight the boy she would most like to have wash her face, trains her pet cat, makes mud-pies and doughnuts —such boys and girls in all these experiences are prophesying their success in the serious endeavors of later life. The culture power of the adult is measured by the play experience of the child.

The Swimming Pool at the River Bank

Environment and Play

There is another aspect of play almost as important as the one above discussed; namely, its influence upon the mental and physical vigor of adult life. Among the Christmas presents this year for the boys and girls of the Orphanage were about fifty pairs of skates and as many coasting sleds. As I write, fifty or more boys and girls are gliding over the ice pond in all sorts of lines, angles and curves. In learning to balance themselves on skates and to do all of the fancy touches and flourishes, including innumerable falls and sprawls in which growing boys and girls delight, these children are laying up a surplus of physical energy that will serve them well in preserving sound health, bodily vigor, and active limbs when life has become more serious and physically less strenuous.

What is better for growing boys and girls than skating in winter and swimming in summer? One is the poetry of motion, the other a classic among childhood amusements. Our swimming recreation for the past season closed with a water carnival which included contests in swimming, diving and floating. The prize-winner in the floating contest was a little girl who kept afloat three minutes without even a film of water passing over her face. The swimming course was up and down the river beach. As many girls as boys swam the whole course, but the boys showed greater strength in swimming against the current and made the distance in less time than the girls.

In these days of so much sedentary employment and so much ease and luxury, reserve power carried forward from youth is especially important if we would prevent physical degeneracy. Boys and girls who indulge freely in all of the healthful out-door sports of childhood will on account of it be more active, more dynamic both mentally and physically, all their days, and they will have the infinite pleasure of looking back upon a happy childlife. Children thus exercised will be better able to resist disease, nervous prostration, and all the other forms of collapse that follow in the wake of physical weakness.

Our Orphanage hospital was open but five weeks during the first three years of our life in this rural home, and for the past two years it has been closed. During the seven years we have lived in these cottage homes, two hundred children have passed through five winters without any of the forms of contagious sickness requiring hospital treatment. This would have been impossible in our city home and on the congregate plan, where scarlet fever, measles and whooping cough were frequent visitors. In wet, slushy weather there are probably fifty pairs of wet feet every day among the two hundred children. To have it otherwise by curbing or confining the outdoor freedom of the children would no doubt incur a greater risk than the danger from wet feet. Where is the normal child that does not love to play in the water? If he can't get into it at the proper temperature and with shoes off, he will take it cold with shoes on! Our immunity from disease is no doubt due to segregation into cottages, to an abundance of pure air, plenty of plain food, and outdoor exercise—in spite of the wet feet.

One of the greatest delights of children is "playing house," which involves so many of the interests of later life, such as the location, planning, and building of the house, the improvising of furniture, the various departments of home

5 65

industries—cooking, sewing, laundry, care of dolls, receiving calls from neighbors, long dresses, lady-like manners, care of the sick, calling in the family doctor, etc. To carry out such a series of imaginative experiences, along with the building and planning and the various associated industries, requires several days, and sometimes weeks. The child will return to the playhouse again and again, adding a new touch each time, tearing down here and building up there, enriching the original conception with each change, and all the time enjoying the fairyland of his own creation. Such rich, life-giving, mind-expanding play development is impossible to children massed in great numbers and within narrow bounds. Where there are several hundred with equal rights on the common playground, the group for such a continued and co-operative play interest could never get together, nor maintain their integrity as a group, even if once selected by a natural sympathy of interests. Again, older children on the same common grounds might not be in favor of such a performance and would be liable to break up the whole undertaking if once

A Fourth of July Tug-o'-War

begun. The same restrictions that prevent the children in one stage of development from indulging in a rich and interested way their play instinct, will operate in a similar manner against those in other stages of development, and thus the plays of children so situated are brought to an impoverished dead-levelism, empty of all richness of content and void of inspiration—a mere bodily exercise that profiteth little.

The first response of the children of the New York Orphanage to the changed environment which the cottage plan and rural location brought about, was manifested in the new-found freedom of play. Playhouses began to spring up here and there on the spacious grounds with the suddenness of Jonah's gourd. Building material of all kinds, and furniture, including everything from old pieces of carpet to leaky teakettles, were in great demand. Children who were old enough to have passed this stage of play interest, let go their pent-up enthusiasm in these plays of younger children. They attempted to live over again those years during which a cramped environment had inhibited constructive and dramatic plays.

Two Hundred Children

It was as though the wings of their imagination were suddenly given the power of flight and they essayed at once to soar.

There was no common ownership in these playhouses. Each one represented the combined purpose, labor and self-sacrifice of two or more proprietors. Property interests and rights were sharply drawn and respected. This interest alone as a by-product of the playhouse enterprise is of great value to institution children—a point which will be developed more fully in the discussion of the economic training of children.

Playhouses, like kites and marbles, come and go with the seasons. It is a little late in the season for them now, but a dozen or more are at present tucked away in obscure corners of the Orphanage grounds. Some are mere leantos against the fence, others only sheds, while one I just visited is furnished with seats, carpet on the floor, pictures on the wall, some kitchen utensils, and a rude weapon or two showing the pioneer spirit of the proprietors. It was only the other day that a little boy told me with glowing interest how he had been an invited guest to one of them and had

Environment and Play

partaken of its hospitality in the form of roasted apples and chestnuts. No doubt many a royal feast has thus been enjoyed in these banquet halls of the children's own building—feasts of which I have not heard, for not every boy is as frank as the one above mentioned. Maybe it does occasionally lead to the indulgence in some forbidden fruit, to "special arrangements" with the cook, or the pantry boys and girls. That must be reckoned with. Enrichment of the child's life in any direction is sure to bring its temptations. But such evils are usually transitory, and are not weighed against the expansion of mind and growth of soul that arise out of the various centers of interest awakened by these plays.

III

INDUSTRIAL TRAINING

III

THE following extract from a letter which the writer received a short time ago from a member of the board of directors of an orphan asylum, states in a most interesting manner the problem of training children:

"Our children have always had the cottage system, located in the country, each house having twenty children, a housemother and a general servant, except in the house for the largest girls, who do the work themselves. In twenty-seven years, with an average number of one hundred received between three and eight years of age, there have been but ten deaths, and two of these were accidental. For the last few years the children have all gone to the public schools, with marked benefit; but this is my problem: How can we develop in a dependent child a noble spirit of independence and self-reliance? The notable characteristics of our girls who go out from sixteen to eighteen, and the boys at fourteen, are lack of self-reliance, and apparently utter inability to take the initiative in anything, or to assume responsibility, and an absence of any aversion to charity. I realize that a child trained to obey and to have all its wants provided for, is not being developed rightly, and I have ventured to ask you how you meet this question in your institution?"

That orphanage certainly has an enviable health record. It is established on the most approved plan, the cottage plan, located in the country, and its children attend the public schools. What does it lack? The searching question asked by our correspondent indicates that something more than a wholesome environment, good health and a public school education is required in order to train up a child in the way he should go; something more than obedience, physical well-being and school attendance.

Before attempting a complete answer to the above question, let me call attention by way of introduction to a few significant facts involved in the problem. Much more is required of the

Industrial Training

orphan child than of the child brought up in his own home. We expect orphan children to go out into the world at the early age of fifteen or sixteen and make their own way; but the child normally situated in his own home is never cut loose entirely from those deeply interested in him, can always count upon his parental roof as a haven to return to if he should fail in his first ventures at self-support; and he returns to it again and again for a new start whenever failure overtakes him. What proportion of men and women succeed in their first ventures? What per cent of your acquaintances at, say forty years of age, have been uniformly successful? Certainly not a large percentage; and statistics tell us that over ninety per cent of business men fail. Consider this in deploring the failures of orphan children.

Again, what an inestimable influence for success is the inspiration that the normal home lends to the first endeavors of the child to earn his own support; and how reluctant the whole family is to acknowledge that the child has failed; how quick to praise every successful effort and to ascribe failure to conditions rather than to the personal equation. Long before the child enters industrial or commercial life, and while yet in school, he feels this inspiration. But the orphan child must fight his battles alone. He is not an endeared member of a family group, and usually receives but little sympathy in his troubles. He is liable to hear censure only if he fails, and has but few to rejoice with him if he succeeds. These spiritual elements, born of kinship ties and so closely related to success or failure, are so much weightier than material conditions, however favorable, that they cannot be estimated by the same standards.

It is not our purpose, however, to waste much time excusing the failures of orphan children. We would better employ the time solving the problem so clearly stated by our correspondent: how to train orphan children so that they will not fail; "How to develop in a dependent child a noble spirit of independence and self-reliance."

The best school in the world is the school of experience, and the surest method of instruction is the method of experience. The deepest lessons

THE MERRY-GO-ROUND

Industrial Training

of life can be learned by experience only. Our problem then is, how to give the child an experience which will develop in him character, efficiency and self-reliance. That these fundamental elements of successful living cannot be learned from books only, nor in an orphan asylum where the child simply lives, behaves himself, and attends school (a sort of charity boarding house), is apparent to any one who has studied the problem. Daily experience in which those qualities which make for success function, is the only method by which they may be acquired; and this means an industrial and economic training for each child. Men and women are independent and self-reliant in proportion to what they can do and what they have. Our problem then is how to develop industrial and economic power in each child. The girl who can describe in oral or written language a beautiful dress which she has seen has some ability, that which the ordinary school imparts; but the girl who made the dress has the power which carries with it independence and self-reliance. The boy who can draw a picture of an incubator knows something about it, but the boy that can run the incubator and get a seventy-five or eighty per cent hatch out of it, knows the incubator itself. The former may learn his lesson in school, but the latter must go to the poultry yard and develop an experience; the former may belong to a class of learned people designated by Bismarck as "the educated proletariat," the latter is your independent, self-reliant breadwinner.

The academic school teaches the child to answer such questions as "What do you know?;" but the question that life itself puts to him when he leaves the school is, "What can you do?" and his dependence or independence is measured by the answer he makes to that question. If orphan children are to be sent forth to shift for themselves at the early age of sixteen or eighteen years, with no home to return to if failure overtakes them, then it is only fair to them that we so train them that they will not fail. Industrial and economic development must come early with such children.

The industrial training that we want is not simply a work experience. The factory type of

Industrial Training

industry would furnish this, but it does not answer the purpose. The child's work, like his play, must be rich in thought content and interesting to him. In the exuberant nature of the child and the importance of giving it ample expression, lies the chief objection to factory employment. It is not the fact that the children must work and earn a living,—many a great man and woman has done this in childhood, —but rather that factory and mine work are of such a nature as to deprive the child of the opportunity during these growing years of storing up physical development and an easy muscular control. If factory work were not so narrow in its demands upon the physical organism; if it were more like farming, stock raising, horticulture, etc., varying from day to day, and employing the whole child, it would not be so injurious.

Children naturally delight in feats of strength and skill. More than half of the amusements of boys arise from contests and struggles of one kind and another. To prevent this natural outflow of growing energy by confining the child to factory routine eight or nine hours a day, cannot but result in arrested development. The emptiness and monotony of it shrivel the mind as well as the body. A child may be just as constantly employed in school work and home industries, taxing his mental and physical resources more every day, and yet not suffer from it as he will when so employed in factory work. The range and change in home industries from week to week will keep his life interests fresh, and give the all-around development that is wholesome for the growing child.

Recently I was one of six invited guests to a four-course dinner prepared and served by three twelve-year-old girls in one of our cottages. It was the round-up and review of a series of lessons given these girls. A few days ago I saw on one of the tables, gingersnaps and bread made and baked by two thirteen-year-old boys, and nut cakes and rolls made by two girls of about the same age. These are more interesting forms of work and of richer content than factory industries.

You can find institutions in which the children

are required to spend several hours each day in mechanical work, such as running knitting machines or other kinds of factory machinery. They have no interest in the product of their labor except, perhaps, to do the required stint and escape punishment. Such labor does not bring the independent and self-reliant spirit we are seeking to develop; the economic element is also entirely lacking. The industrial and economic interests should not be separated in the child's experience.

Yesterday I paid Cornelius and Harold four cents apiece for chickens they have raised this year. One brought forty-four safely through the perils that beset little chicks, and the other twenty-three. They still have others coming on which are not yet old enough to count and turn over to the institution. Several boys built their own poultry houses last spring and took up poultry raising as a side interest along with their other work. One boy raised six hundred tomato plants from the seed, from which over ninety bushels of tomatoes have already been gathered, and the crop is not all in yet. Eighty boys and girls from nine to thirteen years of age planted individual vege-

Two Hundred Children

table gardens in the spring, from which they turned many a penny by the sale of their produce.

Dorothy, a sixteen-year-old girl, who is maid in one of the cottages and on the payroll as a regular apprentice, was very careless a few days ago and burned to a crisp the leg of lamb which she was roasting for the children's dinner. For this piece of expensive carelessness she was required to go to the market, three miles away, pay her own carfare, and buy with her own money another leg of lamb to replace the spoiled one. It took about a quarter of her month's wages to do this, but the lesson was worth ten times that amount, and will, no doubt, return to her a hundredfold in days to come, whatever her occupation may be.

These boys and girls—janitors, storekeepers, gardeners, housecleaners, cooks, etc.—are working and going to school. They are laying the foundation for independent self-support at an early age. They are held strictly responsible for the work assigned them, and are fined for, or required to make good, losses resulting from wastefulness, carelessness or neglect. They are im-

Industrial Training

portant, reliable, constituent factors in the successful running of the Orphanage, in which they feel a real interest. This spirit of service and helpfulness sifts down from the oldest to the youngest child and thus pervades the entire atmosphere. In every cottage, every day of the year, older children are made responsible for the care of the younger ones, while these in turn pay back the debt in whatever service they can render. Each cottage is a hive of industry. The small boys and girls, those from seven to ten, all have their little, but regular, duties to perform.

The work in each cottage is divided up among many apprentice hands. Two boys take care of the basement, one runs the furnace, one mows the lawn, one takes care of the poultry, one keeps the hall clean, two look after the sitting room, two the dining room, three handle all of the china, two make the bread, etc. These duties are performed daily, and through them a sense of responsibility is developed. When an older child is placed out there are prompt applications for the position made vacant. Out of such an atmosphere and experience I do not see how a child can emerge industrially inefficient and irresponsible.

But a child whose institutional life has been that of a charity boarding house, whose needs have all been supplied without his thought or care, who has been taught to obey the dull routine of keeping within bounds, to "wash up" in a row, pray in a row, line up for meals, to retire at night and rise in the morning upon signal, to attend school automatically, to do a little work at irregular intervals, just enough to make him look down upon it and hate it,—such a child at fifteen or sixteen may well answer the description quoted from our correspondent at the beginning of this chapter.

The child is father of the man, and we must put into the formative period of his young life what we expect to draw out later on. It must be put there by experience, not by rote, nor by formal instruction nor by the method of "wise saws and modern instances."

The child must actually do those things which he is expected to perform in a larger way in adult life. He should do them in such a manner as to acquire those elements of character which we look for in the honest, industrious, self-reliant man or woman.

Some visitors to this old New York Orphanage have criticized a charity which provides such beautiful cottage homes, well furnished with modern educational and industrial conveniences, for children from the slums or homes of extreme poverty. These critics have said that it is a mistake to provide such homes for children who will in a few years return to their poor relatives or go to homes so far inferior to the Orphanage home. This criticism would certainly be valid if the children who live here were simply here to have something done for them; to be fed and clothed and sent to school. But the training they receive here does not give them that view of life. They realize that they are here to do something for themselves and in doing it to render a service to others; that a wholesome amount of work lies at the very foundation of things, and that the independent earning of one's living is a worthy ambition for every boy and girl. With this training, much of which arises out of the care and labor necessary to maintain in good order the splendid equipment above mentioned, these beautiful homes with their well-appointed furnishings are not wasted on the children who live here and are taught to take care of them.

Such an environment furnishes the child with a whole group of ideals and standards of living which he will strive to realize later on in his own home. If fortune should cast him back into the slums he will not live the slum life; he will not use his bathtub for a coal bin. The observer, therefore, who thinks this superb equipment will but unfit the child for the environment which he must enter hereafter, sees but hastily and superficially. In fact, he does not see the institution at all; he sees only the plant, the laboratory in which we do our work.

But notwithstanding all this industrial training upon which we depend so largely for the development of the independent, self-reliant spirit, the formal intellectual training of these children is not neglected, as may readily be seen by comparison of our standards of scholarship with those maintained in the public schools.

Every teacher knows what a large per cent of

Our Laundry School

Industrial Training

time in school is wasted on account of want of interest and relish on the part of the pupils. A wholesome amount of industrial activity aids in providing this relish. But it does more than this; it gives the child an appreciation of the value of time, which contributes most helpfully to his schoolroom work. We all know the strength and worth of the student who makes his own way, as compared to the one who feels no such responsibility.

Mabel is seventeen years old. She is ambitious for an education; she has passed through our elementary course and now attends the public high school. During the summer vacation she served in one of the cottage kitchens for several weeks, and later ran the laundry during the vacation of the regular laundress; she earned good wages. When school privileges come at such cost they are pretty sure to be well used and to yield safe returns for the investment of time and labor.

Laura is now a third-year student in the Northfield Seminary. Last summer she served as assistant in one of our cottages and earned good wages. Leonard and Arthur are in the second

Two Hundred Children

year of the public high school, and are also the janitors of our Orphanage school building, for which work they receive a monthly wage.

Several of the boys and girls past fourteen years of age in the Orphanage earn their school time each day by the prompt performance of the industrial work assigned them.

Range in work is as important as range in play. The girls of our Orphanage learn to mend and darn; to make their own clothes; to clean and take care of a house; to cook, to serve in pantry and dining room; to do laundry work and chamber-maid service; to raise poultry; to cultivate flowers, raise garden vegetables, and to take care of younger children. Our boys receive three years' instruction in the use of simple carpenter's tools, learning to make all kinds of useful articles about the home. They learn to chop wood, to use a hoe, shovel and various other garden implements; to make bread; to do practical gardening, and to care for hotbeds; to drive and take care of horses and to raise poultry. The smaller boys learn to clean and dust the rooms of their cottage; to polish the floors; to do dining room, pantry and laundry work; to darn their own stockings, and to sew on buttons. A few of them learn to cook.

In "Up From Slavery," Booker T. Washington tells of his examination for admission to Hampton. It was the task of cleaning a room. He rose to the occasion. He swept it three times and dusted it four times. The examiner of his work was a "Yankee" woman who took out her handkerchief and rubbed it on the walls and over the table and benches. Unable to find one bit of dirt on the floor or a particle of dust on the furniture, she quietly remarked, "I guess you will do to enter this Institution." What per cent of our boys and girls who enter the high school could pass an examination like that, or in fact do any piece of handwork as thoroughly? And yet, does formal education into which American children are thrust almost as soon as they are out of the cradle give any better foundation for character and responsible citizenship than the training that would enable a child to pass such an examination?

For boys and girls who must at an early age become self-supporting, such training is indispensable. Thorough hand training is a good accompaniment of thorough mental training. But there is this difference in doing the work: the mistakes of hand work are easily detected; there is a precision and concreteness about the product of hand work that leaves little or no doubt as to its quality and standard. It is done right or it isn't done right, and there is no question about it. Mental work is not so sharply defined; the mental status of the pupil is not so easily determined. "Bluff" is a common term heard in the classroom among students. It is not so easy to "run a bluff" in the practical forms of hand training. It requires but a moment for the immaculate handkerchief in the hands of a "Yankee" school-ma'am to sweep an obscure corner, and then to say, "You'll do," or "You won't do."

In the training of children, hand work and head work should go together and rest upon the same basis. That is, they should both have a place in the training of the child, for educative, not economic reasons. We have no more right to ask concerning the hand work required of the child, "Is it economic?" than we have to ask the same question of his regular school work. We certainly do not think of asking such a question in the latter case. Hence, the whole range of domestic duties, tasks, and responsibilities above enumerated must be viewed by those in charge from an educational not an economic standpoint. The question is not how much does it cost, or how much expense is saved; but rather, is it educative, and in what way must it be done to best serve the child.

Herein lies one of the important distinctions between children's work rightly regarded and "child labor." There is nothing wrong with the principle of requiring children to work. In fact it is wrong not to have them work; and no doubt ten children come to grief and harm because of idleness to every one that is injured by overwork or unsuitable work. Think of the waste, not to mention the mischief and crime, that result from the unemployed hours of hundreds of thousands of children in our large cities who have no hand work of any kind to do, and no responsibilities to meet outside of four or five hours daily of school attendance five days a week. But standing for several hours a day in a factory building, watching the monotonous repetition of automatic processes, or sitting on a stool making simple adjustments while the machines do all the work, employing the hands in simple movements for separating, testing, packing, etc., of manufactured articles— all this is not children's work, but child labor, and should have no place in child life. It may contribute a few dollars to the family or institution exchequer, but it is certain to be a soul-shriveling process to the child, and almost barren of any results that might be called educational. Such work is child labor and should be prohibited by the law.

The farmer boy, in his wide range of daily tasks, from milking the cows and feeding the pigs in the morning, to digging the potatoes for dinner, weeding the garden in the afternoon, and finally littering the stalls at night, may expend ten times as much energy as the factory boy, and go to bed tired at night; but it is wholesome work, and out of it all he will get a good deal of fun and no end of physical tone and appetite.

A wide range of experience with the fundamental industries in early life is more important

Industrial Training

now than formerly on account of the highly specialized forms of economic industry into which the young man or young woman must enter when independent self-support begins. The unresourcefulness of multitudes of men in middle life who have spent many years in some highly specialized form of labor, and then lost their positions through strikes, lockouts, or some other disturbance, is apparent to any one who has observed or interviewed the unemployed. The man who has learned to do only one or two things is all at sea when he loses his job, and liable to recruit the tramp army of the country.

Range of experience in early years will also enable the youth to determine with more certainty what vocation in life to pursue, for it will reveal to him some aptitudes that will make the task of deciding what course to follow less difficult.

In conclusion, then, all-round industrial training, touching the foundations of several fundamental industries, is a fit complement to an all-round play experience; and together they form the safest background for responsible citizenship and a prosperous career that young people can have.

IV

ECONOMIC TRAINING

IV

THE dominant interest of society in this age is the economic interest. Whether this ought to be so or not, it is so. As soon as the dependent child is sent forth from the institution or the foster home he becomes the victim of this consuming passion of the times. Unless he has had special training to protect him from being exploited for economic ends, he will be little better than a slave in the "home" in which he serves.

When I was a boy living on a farm in Illinois, I knew a youth some six years my senior who was apprenticed to a well-to-do farmer in the neighborhood, and who attended school very irregularly for a few weeks in the winter season. He was known as "one of them New York boys," sent out West because the great cities of the East were congested and there was then, as now, a demand for boys who could work on the farm. I remember what a hard worker this boy was; how early and late, summer and winter, he was the standby help of the farmer with whom he lived. The hired men came and went. They were paid off and gotten rid of as soon as the fall work was done, but this boy wintered and summered year after year with the farm, taking care of the farmer's stock in the winter, ploughing, planting and harvesting his crops in spring and summer. He was neither a hired man nor a member of the family, although he always said "our" in speaking of the farmer's property. He ate and slept with the hired men, but didn't go to town with them Saturday nights nor to the neighborhood frolics at which money must be spent.

There were other boys similarly situated in adjoining neighborhoods. The general conditions of apprenticeship in most cases were, that the boys should receive a new suit of clothes, a horse, saddle and bridle from the farmer when they attained the age of twenty-one years. A liberal estimate for this outfit would be not above one hundred and seventy-five dollars. It could be much less according to the disposition of the farmer in each case. Sometimes the terms were a horse, saddle and one hundred dollars. Whatever it was, it

Economic Training

represented from six to eight years of service, with no money compensation during these years and no spending money, unless by way of a gift now and then,—a form of generosity to which farmers are not greatly addicted. Regular farm hands in the community received from eighteen to twenty-two dollars per month. A moment's calculation will show the extent to which these poor boys were the victims of the parsimonious greed of their employers.

Following is an extract from a letter from one of the boys of a New York orphanage, who was placed on a farm in the West several years ago:

"I went to Nebraska, worked for a man about seven years expecting to get something when I became of age, but got nothing. I was turned out and went to work for another farmer. I had a hard time until last year, but now I am getting a start."

An average boy placed on a farm at fourteen or fifteen years of age should be earning wages by the end of one year. The easiest being in the world to exploit for selfish ends is an orphan child, and no arrangement suits the people who will do this like the long term indenture, with so much to be given when the child attains the age of twenty-one years. A new suit of clothes, a horse, bridle and saddle, etc., are terms of sufficient elasticity to serve such employers of children most admirably. After several years of service have been extracted from the child, there is still time enough left to haggle over the terms of compensation, and to find all manner of fault with the boy's conduct, disposition and general failure to meet the standard of the employer, which is that of a regular farm hand or servant with the one important factor of a monthly wage left out.

There is no arrangement of apprenticeship that sifts so practically and successfully the applicants for the employment of boys and girls in the home and on the farm, as a written agreement specifying a fixed monthly wage, and the privilege of either party to terminate the contract whenever the services of the child on the one hand, or his treatment, on the other, are not satisfactory.

Thousands of orphan boys and girls have become the easy prey of tight-fisted farmers or housekeepers who want a sixteen-year-old child

Economic Training

to do a man's or woman's work for board and clothes. Letters like the following are frequently received by superintendents of orphanages:

"Dear Sir:—We want a little girl about twelve years old to do light work about the house and tend the baby. My family consists of my husband, myself, and three children. We want a girl that we can take right into our family and treat her as one of the children. We will give her good care, feed and clothe her."

Any person who knows human nature, and is familiar with the conditions and relations of family life, knows that nine of such letters out of every ten spell out in actual experience just two words, namely, "white slave." Such applicants want a nurse girl, a dishwasher, a waitress and an all-round maid at the cost of three meals a day and a few work dresses and aprons.

A year or two ago I met a young woman, formerly the ward of an orphan asylum, who had been placed out in a home near New York City when fourteen years of age. She had remained with the same family until the time I met her, when she was twenty-two years old. She was then receiving seven dollars per month and there were fourteen in the family including the boarders. She told me she did all of the cooking. When I told her what wretchedly low wages she was working for and that I could easily and at once get her a much better place, she answered with great concern, "But what would Mrs. —— do without me? I don't believe she could possibly get along." All these years she had been looking out for Mrs. ——. It had apparently never occurred to the girl to look out for herself—the very principle upon which Mrs. —— was acting in exploiting the labor of this poor, ignorant young girl.

The following extracts are from a letter received from one of the boys of this Orphanage who was anxious to go West when fourteen years of age and was given his own way. After working for the farmer with whom he was placed for nearly two years for his board and clothes, he left to work for another farmer at fifteen dollars per month. He remained there four months, drew his wages and returned to the Orphanage. He is now, at seventeen, working for a gardener at sixteen dollars per month. His western experience did him a world of good, but only because he was too wise to be imposed upon for a longer period, by those for whom he worked; otherwise, he would probably have remained until twenty-one years of age, "expecting to get something." The following is his statement:

"The boys are taken by the farmers on condition that they work for board and clothes. Very few of them stay their term out because the farmers will not treat them right. When the boy leaves at seventeen or eighteen he always goes and works for someone else and usually gets from twelve to fifteen or eighteen dollars a month and board. In regard to clothing, I must say it is very small. I never knew any of the boys to get more than one suit a year. I went without underclothes, and all summer without shoes, and very rarely had any socks at all. During the summer a boy gets up between half past four and five o'clock and usually gets through work about eight o'clock in the evening. A boy will get from six to eight weeks' schooling a year and he is not obliged to attend. Enclosed you will find a report showing how many days I went to school."

Two Hundred Children

The report shows two months' attendance, or rather, two months with name on the register. First month present eighteen days, absent five, second month present two days, absent fifteen. The following paragraph from the letter is a wise observation:

"I really do not think a boy has much chance out West, although I am not sorry I went because I can now appreciate a good thing."

There is little doubt that such an experience if it could be terminated in two years, as in this case, would be valuable for most boys born in the city. The question is how to train boys and girls while in the Orphanage or in their own homes so that when sent forth they cannot be exploited for mercenary ends, or made to serve without wages beyond the period when the value of their time and labor should accrue to their own economic advantage. It can be done only by giving the child such an economic training as will put the means of protection within him, in his own views of economic relations; in other words, safeguard him against exploitation by an intelligent comprehension of the relation of work and wages. While he

Apple Picking in the Fall.

Economic Training

is still a child, lift him above the mere brute service of "the man with the hoe."

The only practical training which will prepare the boys and girls to look out for themselves after they leave their orphanage home is a work and wage experience while there. In this Home we are paying over eight hundred dollars a year to the children of the Orphanage for work that they do, as cooks, laundresses, seamstresses, gardeners, janitors, etc. There is no charity in this. We do not pay for work which we would not otherwise be obliged to hire done, nor do we pay more than it is worth.

This work started with the forming of a cobbling class among the older boys. After a dozen lessons by a competent teacher they were able to take up the cobbling work of the Institution. Cut soles and heel pieces were purchased for them and they were paid ten cents a pair for putting on soles and heels, seven cents a pair for putting on soles, and from one to three cents for patching holes. At the close of the month each boy rendered in proper form his bill for the number of shoes repaired. Several boys who earned money in this way opened savings bank accounts. One of the pass books of a member of this first cobbling class begun eight years ago is still at the Orphanage. It shows an average deposit of one dollar a month for fifteen months. It is the beginning of savings on the part of a boy who three years later was placed out on a regular wage per month, and who after serving his employer three and a half years had saved enough to take a course in the Mt. Hermon School for Boys, where he now is.

The economic training given the boys and girls at this Orphanage involves four factors: how to earn money, how to save money, how to spend money, and how to give money. The wage-earning positions in the Orphanage and the regular savings banks of the community provide for the first two. A list of purchases stands over against the scale of wages. Thus, if a girl is receiving a wage of three dollars per month, she must buy her under-wear, shoe laces, handkerchiefs, combs, hair ribbons, tooth brushes, aprons, hose and shoes. If her wages are four dollars per month she must add hats to the above list; if four and a half shirtwaists, and so on up to seven dollars, when she must purchase all of her wardrobe. She may make these purchases alone or with the help of the dressmaker, cottage mother or any older person whose advice she wishes to ask. She may purchase the goods from the Orphanage store if there is in stock what she wants, or she may go to the stores of the city. The important thing is that she shall have a buying experience. No one ever learned to buy in any other way. In buying alone a child sometimes gets "taken in," which is often a valuable experience, but not so disastrous when it comes in child life as it may be in later years. A short time ago one of the boys told me he had been badly "taken in" on his hair-cut, for which he had paid twenty cents. He said he did not know it was "such a bum cut" until he appeared on the playground and the other boys began to "guy" him on it. The next time he will probably not simply have a hair cut but will give directions as to how he wants it done.

Oranges, bananas, nuts and candy are frequently on sale at the Orphanage supply store. The desire for these awakens a money interest in the children who are too young to earn a regular monthly wage.

Two Hundred Children

But many a penny is earned by pulling weeds, sawing wood, sifting coal from ashes or spading up garden plots, and then turned into the fruit or candy counter to sweeten up a Saturday afternoon with a younger brother or sister.

Each child earning a dollar or more a month is required to keep an itemized expense account and submit the same for inspection each month. Following are two pages copied, one from a boy's, the other from a girl's expense book:

Wages received	$4.25	
Missions		.05
Lunch		.20
Deposit in Bank		2.00
Missions		.10
Carfare		.10
Candy		.05
Soda		.05
Show		.10
Hair cut		.10
Fruit		.05
Bananas		.05
Carfare		.10
Two pairs socks		.25
Tie		.25
Two collars		.25
Violin music book		.40
Violin string		.15
	$4.25	$4.25

Economic Training

Wages received	$4.50	
Balance forwarded	.32	
Deposit in Bank		$1.00
Pictures		1.00
Balance paid on suit		.50
Missions		.20
Candy		.10
Fruit		.08
Stationery		.10
Material for shirtwaist		.82
Necktie		.10
Pins		.10
Debts		.10
Treat		.05
I. A. H. Ring		.25
Stamps		.07
Carfare		.20
Balance on hand		.15
	$4.82	$4.82

These expense accounts offer opportunities for many practical lessons in spending, saving and giving money.

The boys and girls of this Orphanage have for several years supported a native orphan child in a mission school in Calcutta maintained by the Woman's Union Missionary Society. Letters are received from her or her teachers from time to time showing her standing, progress in school, etc. This provides for the wise giving of money.

Two Hundred Children

One can easily discover in these expense items certain tendencies which may be corrected at the very beginning of the child's experience with money. The spendthrift, the miser, the reckless buyer, the easy borrower and the careless lender, all reveal themselves in this all-round money experience. One of our older boys loaned three dollars to a stranger, a new employee on the place, last winter. The man remained but a short time and left without repaying the loan. It was a good lesson for that boy and all others on the place. Better to lose three dollars on a careless or unsecured loan at fifteen years of age, however, than a hundred or a thousand times that sum in later years when the responsibilities of life rest more heavily upon the lender.

All this is what we mean by putting the economic safeguards within the child. With such an experience and training in earning, spending, saving and giving money, the orphan child will not serve his employer for a half dozen years "expecting to get something," nor for many months without knowing what wage he is to receive and insisting that it be paid over to him when it is earned.

Economic Training

The following is an exact copy (except the proper names) of a letter received last August from a home in New York in which an orphan boy had been placed some two years previous. It is interesting as a literary production, showing in a measure the grade of culture of homes into which some children are placed.

August 15 1909
R——— S——— Co N Y

Mr. L,—

Dear friend i thought i would rit you a few lines to you to find out wheather Johnny Doe has come there he run a way a week a go last thursday and we would be glad to now wheather he come out there or not i went to lodge and he run a way my women sed he took the cous to pasture he told he was a goanto go and dig out a wood chuck she set up and hunted for him till 11 oclock and then she went up in his room and found his cloths all gone so when i come home she told me he had run a way i supose if he is there he has told you people lots bad but you folks dont want to believe any thing he says for i can send you 10 persons will say they wont believe Johnny under oth we had awful times with him ever sence last febuary he stole a nife and a lot of hens eggs he sold the knife and made us a lot of trouble thay com prety near sending him to bath Jail he is aful light fingurd if he is there you want to look out for him

and if you want me to send these people to send ther
names thay will all sine a paper we tryed to make something out of him i had ordered a new suit of cloths for
him but i was putting him of for to see if it would
be a good boy but he had some one to set him up i
wish you would find out who set him up and oblige me
and rite and let me now if you can i will send a stamp so
you will please let me now wheather he is there or not
from mr and mrs

J. W. Blossom

R————

S————

Co

N Y

R F D no 1

This letter is not introduced here as an argument
against the placing out method of caring for
dependent children, but only to call attention to
the fact that even at the present time important
features are sometimes overlooked by placing
out agencies. The best that an institution can do
for children is not as good as a *good* home. But
good homes, open to dependent children, are not
found without diligent search by competent in-
vestigators. And it is as important to demand a
reasonably high standard—moral, industrial and

Economic Training

intellectual—of the family homes into which children are to be placed, as it is to require a like standard of institutional homes.

If this boy, who was in his sixteenth year, had received a monthly wage, though small, and possessed a little property, if only a pet pig, rabbit or chicken, he would in all probability not have run away from even such a home. With boys, as with men, a little property attaches them to a given locality and makes them more amenable to discipline. That suit of clothes loomed up too hazy in the dim distance to exert a restraining influence upon the boy's wanderlust.

V

THE SCHOOL

THE BOYS LEARN TO DARN

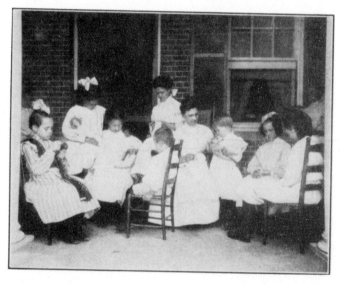

A HAPPY HOUR WITH THE HOUSE MOTHER

V

S HOULD an institution for dependent children maintain its own schools, or send its wards to the public schools?

In favor of the public schools it may fairly be claimed that they keep the child in touch with the world outside the institution; that they place before him standards of competition and scholarship higher than those he is likely to find in the institution because of the great number and range of competitors; that they give him views of social life, ideas of dress, personal appearance, manners and behavior of the ordinary child; that, in fact, they conventionalize his whole life and make him more like other children, so that after leaving the institution he will not forever be marked as an institution-bred child. The playground of the public school furnishes a wider range of personal contact, imparts to him truer and broader notions of civic rights and duties, and thus greatly aids in making an American citizen of him.

Two Hundred Children

All of this is good and not easily matched or overbalanced by any advantages which may be claimed for the institution school. But we may go still further: our public schools are progressive. No student who has carefully followed the changes in the curriculum for the past twenty-five years will deny that the public schools in this country have made great progress. The course of study has been undergoing constant expansion and enrichment in its adaptation to modern life; methods of instruction have become more natural and rational; the standard of preparation for the teacher's work, both academic and professional, has constantly advanced; education has become almost a science and as such has found a place in the curricula of practically all of our universities, while the number of normal schools and teachers' training classes has greatly increased. In addition to all these considerations, it is an inspiration for the children of an institution to be in touch with such a great unifying and Americanizing educational system. In New York state especially, where the standards of the public school system are let down from the top by a body of experts like our state regents, it is important for the dependent child to feel the uplift of this great system.

On the other hand, it may be said that dependent children must have a training somewhat different from that offered by the public schools. The educational problem in their case is much more definite than it is in that of the ordinary child. It is certain that these children must make their own way in the world at the early age of fifteen or sixteen years. A large percentage of such children are below grade in school work, due to irregular school attendance before entering the institution, to poverty and neglect on the part of the parents, to want of medical or surgical attention, or to hereditary handicap. Placed out from the institution at an early age, it is certain also that they will be obliged to make their way in the world by the work of their hands rather than by their wits. Hence their education must be especially strong on the industrial side; they must learn to do things.

Notwithstanding all that has been said above in favor of the public schools, it nevertheless remains true that their curriculum is bookish, abstract and out of touch with the hum of modern life. The growing child would rather do something than stand still and think about it. Growing pains seek relief in enlarged physical function. I believe there is only one remedy for this situation and that lies in the direction of vocational training and a curriculum that takes account of what is going on in the community and spends less time on remote interests and abstractions. The public school curriculum is the "hand-me-down" suit of twenty years ago, before the ready made clothiers furnished the slims and stouts, the longs and shorts of the modern clothing emporium. The institution school, deals with the dependent child only. Its curriculum may become the tailor made suit, the suit that fits. Probably not more than one institution in fifty really provides such an educational fit or makes any attempt whatever to adjust its school curriculum to the particular needs of its wards. For this reason it would probably be better for the forty-nine to send their children to the public schools. But that a much closer adjustment to the needs of

GETTING ACQUAINTED WITH BIDDY'S FAMILY

The School

the child is possible under a wise administration of the institution school, no student of the problem will question.

The advantages of the institution school over the public school lie just here. Between the public school work and the life of the child outside of the school there is a great gulf fixed. This need not be so, but it is so. The institution school can easily bridge this gulf, for since the institution maintains the school and also furnishes the environment for the child's life, it is possible to work up into educative material in the classroom the experience and observations of the child outside the school.

The child should also have along with his more formal education a thorough training in the home-making industries. In this Orphanage, girls are taught to cook; not simply to do a little mincing play sort of work, under the eyes of the teacher, such as one so often sees in cooking school classes, but to prepare the regular meals for the cottage living. To round up three or four courses and to bring them together at an appointed time in the form of a good square meal, is a very different

Two Hundred Children

proposition from participating as one of a half dozen or more pupils in the preparation of two or three courses in the cooking class, where the teacher stands by and tells the child when the bread is ready to go in or come out, how to combine and stir in the elements that make a good cake, or what time to put the potatoes on. To do such work well requires much more time and experience than the public school with its general course only, its "hand-me-down" educational suit, gives to it.

Experience and responsibility are the chief factors in the education that prepares boys and girls for independent self-support at the early age of sixteen. The girl must not only learn the theory of cooking but she must do a good deal of it; she must not only learn how to make her own clothes but she must make them; not only how to launder her own clothes but must have daily or weekly experience in doing it; not only how to repair and change over a garment, but she must do her own changing over for adjustment to growth and fashion, her mending and her darning. The training given our boys in janitor work, house-cleaning, shop work, gardening, poultry raising, etc., has the same fundamental elements of experience and responsibility. The school must adjust itself to this industrial program, which in turn interprets and gives zest to the academic work.

But leaving this industrial side of institutional education, which the public school cannot provide, let us look for a moment at the academic side. Here again there are great possibilities for the institution school to make a better fit than the public school offers. The every-day interests and activities of the child may not only be brought into close touch with the subject matter of the classroom, but may also furnish much of the educative material itself; whereas, the more abstract character of the subject matter of the public school curriculum naturally leaves the knowledge acquired by the child hanging loose and unrelated in his mind. Close and well knit relationships between life and the work of the classroom are usually wanting. This is, and probably always will be, the weak spot in public school education. Much that the child learns is in no way related to his life outside the school. In the institution school, on the other hand, the course of study may be adapted at every turn to the experience and interests of the child. Knowing his daily life so much better than the public school teacher knows the lives of her children, the institution teacher can use to great advantage what the child already knows, to interpret what he is to learn; and thus the apperceptive process may go on much more thoroughly and smoothly; school work is more intelligent and less mechanical.

When asked how long they thought a cow was, a class in one of our city schools measured off about an inch on the index digit corresponding with the length of the little picture of the animal they had seen in their text books. In this case there was need of either an experience that would interpret the lesson, or another lesson better suited to the child's experience. The trouble was simply a misfit.

When the children of our Orphanage school talk about eggs in their arithmetic class, the term is not a mere name, but a definite, concrete idea; not picture eggs, but eggs laid by hens raised on the place, which the children feed and take care of

The School

every day. When they speak of bushels of apples, gallons of molasses, rods of land, tons of coal, etc., they are speaking of objects within the scope of their daily experience. When in the drawing class they make pictures of the rooster, it is the chanticleer they hear every morning in the various cottage poultry yards of the Orphanage; when at Thanksgiving season they draw in color the gobbler, it is the large bronze-feathered bird which they have excited to repeat his jerky and discordant challenge a thousand times by whistling or screaming at him. Pictures of beets and radishes are drawn from the real vegetables raised in their own gardens. The child plants the radish, cultivates the radish, pulls it, brings it to school, paints its picture and then eats it. The donkey they sketch from life has taken them many a ride. The pansies and marigolds they paint were raised in their own flower beds. The bees whose life history they study are working while the children work and in the same schoolroom. The workers coming in laden with the sweets of the flowers, the lazy drones moving about leisurely behind the glass, and occasionally the queen, are familiar objects of interest and study; while the honey itself, the final achievement of the bee enterprise, garnishes the cottage tables and gives the children an abiding interest in these little workers as they "improve each shining hour."

Every important event or development in the life of the home, plowing, planting, cutting down trees and sawing them into lumber and cord wood, starting and running incubators and brooders, buying and selling, building and paving, incidents and accidents,—all are fraught with educative stuff.

Shall we build an ice house? The architect's estimate for a brick structure corresponding to the other buildings on the place is four thousand dollars. With the cost per ton for storing ice in the winter, the present retail price, the allowance for waste in storing ice, interest on the investment, etc., all before them, the children figured out a loss of twenty dollars a year if such an ice house were erected, and we didn't build it.

Our large poultry house needs a new roof. What kind of a roof shall we put on and how much will it cost? Samples of tar paper roofings with prices were obtained. Measurements were taken and estimates of cost made. On the basis of these calculations, with a consideration and discussion of such questions as the difficulty and expense of laying, and the wearing qualities of this or that kind of material, the roofing was selected and put on.

In a similar manner every question of interest that arises in the complex life of the Orphanage makes its contribution to the work of the classroom. Real life everywhere is rich in material of educative worth.

One of our horses is no longer equal to the service we require of him; he is wind broken and has some trouble with his knees, but he is a large fine looking horse and a free goer. A man in Dobbs Ferry has offered us one hundred and twenty-five dollars cash for the horse. Shall we tell him the horse is unsound? After much discussion pro and con in general assembly, it is decided to vote on the question. The result: The girls all voted that we should tell the man that the horse was broken winded and slightly off on his legs, causing occasional veterinary bills; the boys all voted that we should accept the offer and let the buyer take his chances on the deal.

Two Hundred Children

Why the new team was bought in Tompkins County instead of Westchester; what stock they were (Hambletonian strain); what the characteristics of this stock are; the manner in which Dr. L—— of Cornell University examined them to see whether they were sound; what diseases horses are prone to have; how they may be detected; how the horses were transported here in a railroad car; their ages, number of hands high, how many quarts of oats they will consume daily, etc., several makes interesting school exercise.

An accident happens. F. falls from the playhouse high up in a clump of chestnut trees. Both bones of his leg just above the ankle, and the humerus close to the elbow, are broken. In order to set the bones the doctor takes X-ray photographs of the fractures. Extra copies are taken for the school and the children begin their study of the accident with the aid of a manikin. They make drawings of the portion of the anatomy involved in the accident. One or both of two serious results may follow the healing of these fractures. First, they are so near the joint in each case that healing may be followed by a stiff joint;

second, they are in that part of the bone shaft
where elongation takes place in growth and therefore may interfere with further growth, leaving
the boy, when he becomes a man, with two short
members. The study also includes a history of
how the house in the tree came to be, who built it
and who the original proprietors were, how many
times it has changed hands and at what prices.

A case of diphtheria appears in the Orphanage.
It immediately suggests a whole troup of ideas
which are taken up with the work in physiology
and English. What kind of a disease is it, how
does it spread, and what must we do to protect
ourselves against it? How a culture is taken,
how it is developed, what antitoxine is, how it is
obtained, pictures of the laboratory in which it is
produced, description of the horses used for this
purpose, manner in which it is preserved, cost
of it, how it is administered, how much is a dose;
also, how the children felt when they saw the
instrument for administering antitoxine, how they
felt the next day, what is the theory of its use
as a medicine, how it gets into the system by
hypodermic injection, etc.,—all constituting a

network of related studies of practical, every-day interest and worth.

Eighty boys and girls are following step by step the new cottage now being erected on the grounds of the Orphanage. The various kinds of material, from the drain tile of the foundation to the slate on the roof are examined, and the cost and use of each are entered up in the child's record of the work.

Will Carlton is engaged to lecture to the children. Immediately the teachers of the four upper grades in English turn their attention to a study of the coming lecturer and his works. His biography is learned, his most popular poems are read and choice selections taken from them and committed to memory. His beautiful Decoration Day poem, "Cover Them Over With Beautiful Flowers," is memorized and sung. By the time the lecturer comes, every child is interested to see and to hear him.

So it would be easy to continue indefinitely these examples of correlation of school and home life. The quantitative relations involved in carrying on the work of the Orphanage form much of the arithmetic of the classroom; the record

The School

of daily experience, much of its English; and the two, the school life and the home life, are knit together by innumerable criss-cross strands which vitalize the one and interpret the other.

There is another important aspect in which the institution school can adjust itself to the needs of the child and where the public school fails to meet a condition. As children move upward through the grades the subject matter of instruction grows more and more abstract, while the child, in the earlier years of the adolescent period, the years of physical stress and rush, unless naturally studious or academic in his tastes, yearns for concrete experience, for action, for industrial work and freedom from physical restraint. In the institution he may give half of each day to industrial work and the other half to school work, thus preserving a balance that may tide the child over a restless period of a year or two and still preserve and keep alive and going those academic interests which ordinarily are lost forever to the pupil that drops out of the public school during these years.

In one of the smaller manufacturing cities of Massachusetts where I lived for several years, the boys and girls in the grammar grades of the public school were constantly dropping out, as soon as their age and school attainments fulfilled the requirements of the law, to enter the various mills and factories of the town. During the four years of my official connection with one of the largest manufacturing concerns of the place, I sent hundreds of visitors through the factory, who were anxious to see the changes through which various forms of raw material pass on their way to a finished machine. Not one school teacher of the community ever asked for such a privilege, although there were five hundred within a radius of five miles. The same could be said concerning the large cotton mills of the city. In the schools the children were memorizing facts about the production, manufacture, and use of cotton, wool, steel, rubber, leather, etc., the very materials that were being shaped into finished product by most interesting processes in great industrial enterprises within sound of the school bell. The natural and rational curriculum for the child was in the life of the community; and there was no lack of material for such a curriculum.

The School

It was said of Ephraim of old, "He's joined to his idols, let him alone." Books are the idols of most school teachers; they are joined to them and want to be let alone. Why shouldn't the boys and girls of such a community drop out of school as soon as allowed to? They want life and want it more abundantly than they find it in the schoolroom. The life interests of the community are the life interests of the family. The parents and older brothers and sisters talk about the mill and factory work, wages, rents, savings, purchases, sales, etc. The younger children become interested and yearn for a place in the industrial life of which they see and hear so much. The relation between their school work and the interests of the community is so remote that they are unable to see any advantage to themselves in continuing school after they are old enough to take a wage-earning position. Such a condition need not exist and will not when we infuse into the mummified curriculum of "modern" education the life-blood of the industrial, economic and social interests of the here and now.

133

VI
PUNISHMENT

VI

VISITORS to this old New York Orphanage, especially those who are officially connected with other institutions for children, frequently ask the question, "How do you punish your children?" After putting the same question in a letter which I received a short time ago from one of the trustees of an institution for orphan children, the writer said, "I am ashamed to tell you how we punish our children; it is so barbarous."

The chief qualification of the old time schoolmaster was the ability to keep order. This usually meant plenty of corporal punishment. My memory vividly recalls an experience, less than two score years ago, in a district school, in which I saw fifteen pupils whipped in one half day. A common object of interest as we entered the school-house each morning was two or three long "gads" reposing on nails driven in the wall

behind the teacher's desk. The fundamental pedagogical principle in The Hoosier Schoolmaster
was, "no lickin', no larnin';" and Irving has the
schoolmaster of Sleepy Hollow "administer justice
with discrimination rather than severity; taking
the burthen off the backs of the weak, and laying
it on those of the strong. Your mere puny
stripling, that winced at the least flourish of
the rod, was passed by with indulgence; but
the claims of justice were satisfied by inflicting
a double portion on some little, tough, wrong-
headed, broad-skirted Dutch urchin, who sulked
and swelled and grew dogged and sullen beneath
the birch."

Whittier presents a very different type of
schoolmaster in his Snow Bound, but nevertheless introduces him as the "brisk wielder of
the birch and rule," and Goldsmith says of his
schoolmaster:

"Well had the boding tremblers learned to trace
The day's disasters in his morning face."

All this has now passed away and the pendulum
has swung far to the other side of the arc. So

Punishment

impressed with the riot of liberty that has followed the abandonment, of the rod as an instrument of punishment, was the president of a
certain normal school, whom I knew a few years
ago, that he was accustomed to remark in his
talks to parents and teachers, "Thousands of
boys in this country today are going straight
to the devil for want of a good Christian licking."
It is a pretty safe proposition to make, but it
is also probably true, that there are usually other
and wiser ways of obtaining the desired results
than by the use of corporal punishment.

The old definition of punishment in our elementary pedagogy was about as follows: "Punishment is pain inflicted upon the mind or body
of a person, by the proper authority, either to
reform him, or to deter others, or both." Of
late years many have declared against pain
inflicted upon the body as a form of punishment.
Just why the body, or the epidermis which covers
it, has become so sacred that it must no longer
be the medium through which the will may
become trained, the mind informed or reformed,
does not appear in argument. Such people

usually prefer to rail against corporal punishment rather than give sound reasons for abandoning it.

Some time ago the superintendent of an institution in which corporal punishment was forbidden, told me of a novel substitute for it. When a certain boy was so naughty and disobedient that it became necessary to administer punishment, he was given a sort of Turkish bath, with less soap and more salt and friction than is ordinarily used, thus "toning up" the whole system. This was corporal punishment in disguise and not against the letter of the law.

In forbidding corporal punishment it becomes necessary to define it, but it is difficult to include in a definition every form of bodily chastisement; hence teachers and others who have charge of large groups of children often evade the letter of the law, which does not mention shutting up in the closet, standing on the floor, going without meals, putting to bed, shaking up, or giving "Turkish baths." These are regarded as more refined forms of corporal punishment than the birch switch, the oiled strap or mamma's slipper.

Punishment

The wisdom of our ancestors is in the latter, the ingenuity of our contemporaries in the former.

Corporal punishment is but one form of correction; it is usually the shortest and frequently the least helpful. Its absence because of a higher and better form of punishment is wise and well, but its absence by law or rule is pretty sure to play havoc with the establishment of authority and to work ruin to the children. In other words, there is one thing worse than corporal punishment, and that is a law prohibiting it.

The effect upon teachers or parents who frequently resort to punishment is as serious as upon the child who is frequently punished. In fact, much punishment is a lazy and stupid method of attempting to obtain results. Punishment should be regarded as medicine to be administered to children who are morally sick. A good physician prescribes as little medicine as possible and thus gives nature a chance. He also carefully diagnoses each case and administers the specific remedy required. One great danger in the use of corporal punishment is, that it is considered a cure-all for every form of moral delinquency. The parent or teacher who forms the corporal punishment habit will turn to it with as little thought or little study of the individual case as does a vender of patent medicine, who prescribes his one remedy for every disease of every patient.

As long as we are animal and physical, as well as moral and spiritual beings, government in its last analysis must rest upon a physical basis. The abolition of corporal punishment, therefore, in the training of children, is unsound in theory. Yet he would be a reckless school superintendent, or member of a school board, who would place the power to administer it in the hands of the thousands of teachers in a great school system. This only means that there is great responsibility attached to the use of this means of discipline; and that those in authority are not willing to assume the risk of such a responsibility placed in the hands of so large a number, many of whom are young, inexperienced, or without self-mastery under provocation. Everybody feels better when the home assumes the burden of

such a responsibility. The following illustration
is to the point:

"Manhattan.—Miss —— recently brought four of
her pupils into the children's court for 'behaving like
the mischief.' They were found guilty. Justice ——
looked puzzled and then turned the four boys over to
their mothers, who whipped them."—The School Bulletin. August, 1908.

If the above incident is true, and the chastisement was well and properly administered, it
is certainly a remarkable case—to find four
such sensible mothers. It makes one feel that
"there is a God in Israel" (New York) yet.

Every child has a right to know that there
is such a moral force in this world as authority;
that it is necessary to his well being, and that
it is as unyielding as a law of nature. Not only
has he a right to know this truth, but if he doesn't
know it he must learn it. If the little one seizes
the blade of a sharp knife he is cut; if he thrusts
a stick into a beehive he will get stung; if he
falls on the floor, or the stones of mother earth,
they will not soften to receive him. Thus the
child soon learns not to trifle with the laws of

nature; otherwise his abode here would be but brief. In the same manner he has a right to know by experience that moral law must be obeyed. His natural birthright to such knowledge rests with the family. Unfortunate indeed is his lot if he fails to learn respect for authority in his own home, where love and patience temper the lessons to his tender years.

But in this country there are multitudes of homes in which obedience to authority is an unknown virtue—on the part of the children. (It has been said, however, that there is just as much authority in the American family today as there ever was, except that it has changed hands). After the home the child's next opportunity to meet this indispensable moral force is in school. Alas! here it has also been losing ground for the past twenty years, until it has absolutely disappeared from many schools.

The last and only other opportunity for the child to learn this fundamental principle of government is in society, at the hands of an officer in blue coat and brass buttons, unaccompanied by any exercise of patience or affection, and

Punishment

not unfrequently enforced by the blows of a club. Our poor wayward child at last learns what our sentimental friends, who condemn the symbols of authority honored of our ancestors, forgot; namely, that authority in the last analysis rests upon a physical basis. This is why we appoint large men for policemen and arm them with clubs, build immense battleships protected with heavy armor, and maintain a standing army equipped with repeating rifles and gatling guns. But government at the end of a policeman's stick usually comes too late to be morally uplifting. The youth has passed the period of formative development, and the discipline to which he must now be subjected is that of restraint of person or physical compulsion. It may be reformatory, but in many cases we all know it is not; the individual is simply shut up for the better protection of society.

It may be put down as generally true that wherever punishment is made a prominent feature in the lives of children, self-control and moral standards are at low ebb. Efficient moral character, the goal toward which we work in all our educative endeavors, is an inner structure, not an outward form. Where punishment functions largely, there is certain to be a lack of wholesome incentives to self-mastery and to constructive moral effort.

In order that punishment may not have a large place in the training of children, it is first of all necessary to provide abundantly for their occupation. A child left to his own devices, is a danger signal. To require a child to behave and yet give him nothing to do is cruel. Under such conditions authority is maintained by fear of punishment only. It is entirely external and has but little or no educative worth. To attempt to make punishment take the place of occupation in the training of the child is blundering tyranny; and yet it is just what many parents, institutions, and the courts are doing every day.

The long summer vacation is at hand. Thousands of boys will get into trouble and suffer punishment within the next three months simply because they have nothing to do. Many birds' nests will be robbed, many a mother bird slain or bereft of her young, and many a harmless

WORKING OUT THEIR FINES

Punishment

animal tortured by boys who have nothing else to do; by boys who would just as gladly have made bird boxes and fastened them in the trees, or built cages and made pets of the animals that they tortured, if only someone interested in the boys had provided material and tools, opportunity to earn money to buy them, or perhaps even the mere suggestion that the boys employ their time in this way. The following two items were clipped from newspapers during the long vacation of last year:

"Lenox, Mass.—John, William and James ——, seven, ten and thirteen years old respectively, went to M—— P——, a liveryman, late yesterday afternoon and said their mother wanted a team to drive to Pittsfield. P—— let them have his best horse and buggy. When the rig was not returned early last evening, and it was found that the boys' story was false, Policeman D—— was notified. With several other South Berkshire officers he searched for them all of the day. Late this afternoon they were discovered at Day's Hotel in Otis, twenty miles from Lenox. The trio said they slept out all of last night and were going to 'rough it' for a spell."

"Passaic, N. J.—Four boys have been arrested for attempting to wreck a train near Passaic, and have confessed that it was their sixth attempt of this kind. The only reason they gave was their desire to witness the excitement. Young America in search of excitement is a dangerous proposition and should have his ambition chastened by the reform school."

To any student of child nature, it is apparent that the main cause of such juvenile delinquency is the want of inducement to wholesome forms of activity. These boys were simply left to their own resources for finding interest, excitement or employment, and it is not strange when so left that their energies should manifest themselves in such abnormal and forbidden ways. If the parents of these children, or someone else in the community who was interested in them, had furnished adequate motive for expenditure of their energy along proper lines, they would in all probability not have sought criminal ways for its expression.

When hundreds of thousands of children are turned out of school with no work, no interests or industries of any kind for them to pursue, and no one to safeguard their leisure with suggestions as to how to employ their time, it is not at all surprising that they should run amuck of police officers. Thousands of boys all over the country are thus going the wrong way simply for want of someone to show them a better course and lead them into it. Instead of the blind, blundering view expressed by the short-sighted writer above quoted: "Young America in search of excitement is a dangerous proposition and should have his ambition chastened by the reform school," we should have parents, teachers, neighbors and social workers providing helpful, happy and wholesome ways for the outflow of the pentup energies of boyhood. It is not reforming schools but forming schools that young America needs.

Many of the boys and girls in this Orphanage earn money every month. An interest in money not only motives a large share of their leisure time which would otherwise go to waste or mischief, but it also develops individual initiative and self-mastery, and in this way contributes to moral training. Cut off the opportunity for the thousand and one odd tasks which the boys of the Orphanage are constantly seeking to perform for money, and mischief, ill behavior and the necessity for punishment would at once increase. During the vacation I can scarcely walk across the grounds without from one to half a dozen boys "striking me for a job." It is the cry of surplus energy for profitable outlet. Not to provide for it means its escape in some forbidden channel. Where much occupation is provided, little punishment is needed. It keeps one busy finding occupation for two hundred children, but it is a pleasanter task than devising methods of punishment.

Money responsibility may be used to excellent advantage as punishment and also as a means for the development of moral control. The punishments used in institutions often lose their force by their dreary monotony. After a boy has been whipped half a dozen times, that form of punishment loses practically all its effect as a moral influence or as a painful ordeal, even though the whipping may be a severe one. Read "Tom Brown at Rugby" for examples of this.

In adult society, if one man assaults another, he is fined; if he disturbs the peace, he is fined;

Punishment

if he cruelly treats his horse, he is fined; if he sells impure foods, he is fined. Cash responsibility in the shape of fines is universal. Why, if it works well with men, may it not work well with children? It is certainly as rational a medium in which to express moral responsibility as any other external penalty may be. It has a great advantage over corporal punishment, shutting in the closet, putting to bed, or administering "Turkish baths." In fact, it gives the child something to do rather than simply having something done to him. It lays upon the child a responsibility for his own deed. In earning money to pay his fine, he punishes himself. In our Orphanage we keep a book account of fines and they stand on record until paid. A fine may not be paid for many weeks or months after it has been imposed, but the very fact that there is a responsibility on record, which must be met, exerts a wholesome and restraining influence over the child. Following are representative entries from our fine book:

E. M....Leaving book out in the rain........ .25
R. H....Breaking gas globe................ .25

Two Hundred Children

M. G.....Spilling ink on apron............... .10
I. B.....Playing with matches in basement .. .25
L. L.....Making fudge without permission ... .50
J. D.....Breaking clinic thermometer........ .40
V. J.....Defacing school desk............... .10
A. W.... Breaking little girl's doll........... .10
G. W.....Stealing apples..................... .25
E. K.....Burning apron..................... .10
I. B.....Misusing best suit.................1.00
M. B.....Tearing music...................... .10
F. W.....Destroying hat..................... .10
H. P.....Stoning pigeons.................... .10
W. N.....Taking nails from carpenter shop. .. .10
W. W.....Stealing oranges................... .25

When the boys in Bethune Cottage brought
one of their number to the office with the request
that he be "everlastingly licked" for committing
a piece of vandalism, they expressed the tradi-
tional view of punishment handed down to us
from remote times, and not yet entirely outgrown.
It was the quantitative view—an eye for an eye
and a tooth for a tooth; so much punishment
for so much offense. It is common even now-a-
days to hear parents, teachers, institution caretakers, etc., say, "This child deserves a good
whipping, a sound thrashing," etc. Whereas,

Punishment

it is not a question of what he deserves, but rather a question of what will be most helpful to enable him to overcome, by self-formed purpose or mastery, his desire to repeat the offense.

We do not prescribe punishment for a child that has become ill even through carelessness or disobedience. We do not say anything about what he "deserves," but immediately proceed with the medicine or treatment which will best restore him to health. So should it be if he is morally delinquent, which after all is a kind of sickness. Justice, or what he deserves, in the old sense of the term, has nothing to do with it.

Deprivation is an excellent form of punishment, and we use it frequently in this Orphanage. It obviously cannot be used where there is a dead-levelism of interests, possessions and activities; where there is no scope for individual initiative or enlargement of opportunities. If children have money and property; if they have skates and sleds, bathing suits and wagons, gardens, rabbitries, pigeon-houses, play-houses, fishing tackle and tools; if they have a variety of cloth-

Two Hundred Children

ing, the privilege of making visits to friends, taking trolley rides, or going to town; if their lives are thus enriched, as every child's life should be, then deprivation may become a strong help in discipline and in moral training. Nothing in this Orphanage gets hold of a boy quicker in summer than to be required to leave his bathing suit in the office until his conduct improves. His skates represent almost as large an interest in winter, and nearly every child, old enough to require punishment, has some privilege or possession near enough to his heart to bring pressure to bear on his conduct if it becomes necessary to use it for that purpose. The very possession, however, of all these privileges and instruments lessens the need of punishment.

VII
MORAL TRAINING

VII

EVERY institution has its moral atmosphere and tone. Strong personalities establish the standards and cut the patterns which persist year after year by imitation and repetition. The children come and go, but the institution with its traditions, its moral standards, its rules and regulations, chiseled as it were in adamant, remains. Its molds and dies give shape to all who pass through. Moral training with children is more a matter of atmosphere and standard, of example and imitation than of formal instruction.

The various forms of education and training discussed in previous chapters of this book are shot through with moral relations. These, however, may not appear in the consciousness of the child. It is important that they should appear and that they should exercise a controlling influence; for morality is a quality of character, and not merely a mental acquisition. One may be trained intellectually, industrially or economically without being moral. Character, however, is not made up of separate compartments. Each child is a unit, although a very complex one. If the character is morally sound its expression in every direction—social, intellectual, industrial, economic, etc.—will be moral.

An education which does not rest on a moral foundation is worse than ignorance. The goal of the entire educative process is moral character. Conceding the truth of this proposition, as almost all parents and teachers do, it is remarkable that instruction in morals receives so little attention from them. The National Education Association is the most representative body of educators in the country. In running through the annual reports of the past fifty years of its history, one finds a surprising dearth of matter on the subject of teaching morals. Each branch of the curriculum in its manifold aspects of content and method has been treated again and again, and great progress in the making of a course of study better adapted to the needs of the children and of the times has undoubtedly resulted from these discussions. But instruction in morals has never received extended or intensive treatment at the hands of this great association; and from the present status of moral instruction in our public schools as compared with any former period, it is not easy to see that any progress whatever in this field has been made.

In his paper before the meeting of the National Council of Education at Los Angeles, in 1907, Mr. Clifford W. Barnes, Chairman of the Executive Committee of the International Committee on Moral Training, said, "Generally speaking systematic moral instruction may be said to have no place in our American school system, for it has only been tried to a very limited extent in a few small places."

It is not difficult to see why our public schools have made such indifferent progress in the teaching of morality during the past fifty years. The deterioration of the home as a center of moral influence during the same period is also easily accounted for. Our public school system was established as an adjunct to the home and the

Two Hundred Children

church at a time when both of these institutions stood for much more in the life of the child than they do today. It was established at a time when the child was much less a ward of the state than he is today; when life was rural, and homes were houses and lands, with firesides and gardens, not tenement boxes; when the course of study was rich in the literature of moral and religious truth; when religion was potent in the home, parental authority was unquestioned and the church and the minister functioned largely in every community.

These conditions have all changed. The delinquent child of today is the product of city and town life. Out of one hundred and thirty thousand children in our reformatories, ninety-eight per cent come from cities, towns and villages. In Baltimore, crime is said to be fifty per cent greater in the slum tenement district than in the city at large; in Chicago over two hundred per cent greater.

With the growth of factory industries the home as an industrial center has steadily declined. With the elimination from home life of the old

Moral Training

ashioned chores and daily responsibilities for
ome-making services and industries, has come
he breaking down of family discipline and
arental control. Occupation and behavior must
o hand in hand. Children cannot behave if
hey have nothing to do.

Along with the weakening of home influence
as come an immigration of a million or more
oreigners annually,—parents too ignorant to
earn our language, with children quick to grasp
he privileges of American liberty but without
he sense of self-control or civic responsibility
vhich safeguard it. The result of all these
lisintegrating factors upon child life is not
nly an increase of juvenile depravity, but a
atio of precocious crime and delinquency not
nown a half century ago.

While only a passive agent in the moral deteri-
ration of the home resulting from these social,
conomic and industrial changes, the state has
een an active agent in the elimination of religious
nstruction from the public school. Moral in-
truction in the earlier period of education in this
ountry was inseparably bound up with religious

instruction. But through the gradual drawing away of the public schools from church influence the function of the teacher as a monitor in religious matters has been greatly reduced, the literature of religious truth, as such, excluded from the class-room, and the whole situation secularized to such an extent as to effect almost a complete elimination of religious instruction from public education. This condition has forced a schism between religious and moral instruction, and left the latter swinging in the air. Whether the state could have done otherwise and yet safe-guarded in the public schools our American ideal of freedom of conscience and religious liberty, is a question. Our only purpose here is merely to call attention to the fact. Whatever may be true of the ability of the mature mind to form moral conceptions and act upon moral grounds independent of religious feeling or of the consciousness of a Supreme Being, it is certainly true that such ethical abstractions do not appear to the child mind.

At each step in the elimination of religious instruction from the public schools society, has

Moral Training

assumed increased risk. Public elementary education is the extension downward of the nation's authority by moral suasion. It is the peaceful arm of the police system before it has become necessary to display the blue coat, brass buttons and locust wand. The only rational and adequate means within the power of a democracy to conserve and perpetuate herself, her laws and her institutions, is through public education. We are expending immense sums of money trying to correct grievous ills by legislation. This is attempting to effect social uplift by throwing our weight on the short arm of the lever. It is a thousand times better to form than to reform. The children of today make the state of to-morrow. Nine-tenths of these children receive their education in the public elementary schools. Character by culture through education, instead of by laws and penalties, should be the aim of society. An education which is not moral is unsafe both for the individual and for the state.

Not only is the public school shorn of much of its power for moral instruction by excluding

from it all religious instruction, but it is also
further handicapped as a moral influence by the
fact that ordinary academic instruction does not
offer a large field for moral action. The end
of moral training is freedom. Freedom is liberty
of choice coupled with sufficient moral insight
and self-control to choose the right; for choosing
what is wrong results in a limitation of freedom.
One is free who does as he pleases but pleases
to do right. Moral training is, therefore, not
merely informing the intellect by means of moral
standards and ideals, but it is forming the will
to choose aright. Character has been defined
as a perfectly formed will, but it must be under
stood that the principal agent in forming the
will is the will itself. The will, building character
by its own conscious acts, is the supreme aim
of moral training.

The child that is trained up "in the way he
should go will not depart from it," because his will
has become morally formed and he does not
choose to. How to provide the child with a
moral experience rather than simply moral ideas
is the problem we have to work out in moral

Moral Training

training. We all distrust direct moral instruction, and yet in our public schools are scarcely
able to furnish an environment that contains
anything worth while in the way of moral experience. The point of contact between teacher
and pupil is intellectual and academic rather
than moral and practical.

School life as the child finds it is forced and
artificial. It is not real life and the child knows
it. The material with which the school deals
is remote from the child's natural interests.
He fails to see its connection with practical
everyday living. He, therefore, does not take
it as seriously and genuinely as he does his life
outside the school. If to him the environment
is artificial, the content of his studies unrelated
to the life about him, the moral standards required of him in the schoolroom will likewise be
merely academic. This rather empty and nega-
tive condition of the public school, with respect to
moral training, would be greatly relieved through
an enrichment of the school curriculum and a
vitalizing of its activities by an infusion of the
warm current of the child's every-day interests

and experiences outside the school. Unless we
are able to do this we must content ourselves
with merely skimming the ground of moral training in public school education.

That which reaches the child through his experience is tenfold more a part of him than
that which comes to him through mere ideas
or sensory stimulus. One moral experience is
worth a score of formal lessons in morality.
One of the boys in our garden class stole
radishes from another boy's garden and was
caught in the act by two or three of his com-
panions. All of the gardeners were at once
assembled; the boy and his case were set before them. After some informal discussion a
motion was made by one of the children that
the boy forfeit his garden. It was one of the
best in the plot and he had spent much time
on it, but by his deed he had violated property
rights and thus forfeited his right to its ownership.
The motion was unanimously carried. When the
assembly was asked if there was any further business concerning the matter, it was moved by one
of the children that this boy be required "to weed

all of the other gardens." This motion was not entertained by the chair, but would no doubt have carried if a vote had been taken on it: first, because recent rains had greatly increased the growth of weeds in the gardens; second, because of natural laziness in relation to such work as weeding gardens; and third, because the thief was an unpopular boy.

Soon after the walls and ceilings of one of the boys' cottages in our Orphanage had been decorated, a boy made with a nail an ugly scratch about ten feet long through the paint on the wall of one of the dormitories. This is the boy referred to in the chapter on Punishment, who was brought to the office by other boys of the cottage with the request that he be "everlastingly licked." But they were shown that there was no connection between the culprit's offence and a "licking." They were then given some instruction as to principles of punishment with special reference to the fact that punishment should bear a natural relation to the offence, and that it should when possible take the form of an indeterminate sentence. The matter was referred back to the boys for further deliberation. The decision reached and presented the following day was that the boy should sleep in the attic, going to bed in the dark, until such time as it was thought safe for him to return to the dormitory. He was kept sleeping in the attic for about six weeks.

Several interesting inferences may be drawn from such instances as these. First, that children are capable of rational action upon moral questions. Second, that it is unsafe to give absolute authority into their hands, as has been attempted in some of our school government schemes; for children are emotional and may be mercilessly cruel in passing judgment and executing moral or governmental functions. Third, that participation in government under proper restriction is an essential factor in the training of the future citizens of a democracy, and that helping to discipline and govern others promotes self-government. Not one case of stealing from gardens has been reported, or to our knowledge has occurred since this case, which happened three years ago. The damage to the wall was repaired and no

Moral Training

similar case of vandalism in the cottage has occurred for about the same period.

Each new boy received into the cottage comes up against a moral leverage with respect to certain home-making refinements, group ideals and industrial standards, which he cannot resist. He is seized and shaped to the molds by forces which he cannot withstand. The same may be true with respect to moral standards in any school if the teacher works wisely and diligently to establish them.

Children, as far as they are able to understand, should be conscious of the process through which they are passing. Nothing will secure their co-operation more surely than to understand your purposes concerning them, the habits which you want them to form, and the principles which you want regnant in their lives. I have found it a good plan to place before them for solution, problems in child training concerning themselves and other children. Attempts to solve such problems lead the child to introspection and self inquiry. You fight the battle alone in training a child if you do not have his conscious co-operation in the work. He is your strongest ally against the foes that are within or the temptations without. A thorough system of discrimination with respect to individual merit or demerit for discipline, scholarship, service rendered, etc., is an important factor in moral training. Nothing is more wholesome and helpful to the child than to know that he stands on his own feet, that he is not merely one of a crowd.

In this Orphanage we endeavor to reward every best effort or excellency in the work and conduct of each child, and to offer numerous opportunities for individual initiative along many lines. This is especially needed in institutional life, where the besetting sin is pretty sure to be dead levelism. Make the boys and girls conscious of this fact, and open ways for them to escape from such a condition, and they will break through the crust of solidarity which may have settled over them like a pall.

Moral training requires that children should be put upon their honor and trusted. Responsibility lies at the very foundation of morality. Children are quick to sense the moral atmosphere in which

Moral Training

they are placed. If it is one of distrust they immediately respond with its natural accompaniment, deception. The less you trust children the less worthy of trust do they grow. It is better to trust and be deceived than not to trust at all. Expect much in this regard and you will get much. Distrust and lack of confidence beget irresponsibility and delinquency. The sense of moral guilt is much keener when the child betrays or abuses a trust than it is if he does wrong when expected to do so if he gets a chance. Wrong doing should be a surprise and not a matter of course.

No more surveillance and coercion in moral action should be exercised than is absolutely necessary. The coercion may not be that of a personal force, but rather that of a system. There should be a progression from younger to older in the matter of responsibility. The playgrounds of our Orphanage are open and unfenced. Our children are not under surveillance while at play any more than are the children of any well-regulated family. A child can run away if he wants to. No one is watching him to see that he does not run away, any more than you would have some one watch your own children in a country home. The boys wander over most of the place (comprising over forty acres) in their play, or after cherries, chestnuts or wild flowers. Every pleasant Sunday afternoon the children take walks into the country. They go in groups of from three to twenty, the girls always accompanied by some older person, the boys usually without escort other than one or two of their own number. Children fourteen years of age or older frequently make visits of several days or weeks to relatives, for we believe in strengthening kinship ties where they are safe and proper. Our children go to New York, Yonkers and Hastings on errands frequently and alone. About fifty weeks of visiting with relatives and friends were among the privileges which the boys and girls of the Orphanage enjoyed during the past year.

Ample opportunity must be provided for the child to exercise freedom of choice whenever consistent with his highest good. Nothing makes for individual responsibility like the exercise of free choice. Since the child will soon be sent forth into the world where he will do all of his own choosing, it is important that he should do some of it now, while under training, as a preparation for that greater responsibility. The child of fourteen should have wider range of free choice than the child of twelve.

The superintendent of a New York institution some time ago received a letter from the people to whom an orphan child fifteen years of age was apprenticed, stating that the child would never take a bath unless made to do so. The regular custom in the institution was two baths a week for all the children. As this child had been in the institution about ten years, it had repeated the practice of bathing about a thousand times and yet the habit of taking a bath had not been formed. In a subjective or psychological sense, however, this child had really never taken a bath. If we analyze the complex process of taking a bath into its elements we note the following: feeling the need of a bath, desire to satisfy the need, choosing the time, manner and conditions for taking a bath, and finally the application of soap and water. With but one of these steps had the child had anything whatever to do during the entire ten years of her life in the institution. Hence the child had not acquired the habit of bathing.

The forming of a habit above the level of mere instinct, requires something more than repetition. If feeling, desire and choice are necessary steps in the act which is to become habitual, they must function in the genetic process of establishing the habit. Without purposeful effort no habit will be formed even by endless repetition. This is why institutionalism is so empty and barren of intelligent response in character and efficiency on the part of those who have been subjected to its stupefying régime.

Public sentiment may become as potent a factor for moral uplift among children as among adults. Almost unlimited possibilities for good lie in this comparatively neglected field in school discipline. Two of my children attended a high school in Massachusetts where there was almost no cheating or cribbing, and what little there was, was frowned upon by the students; the

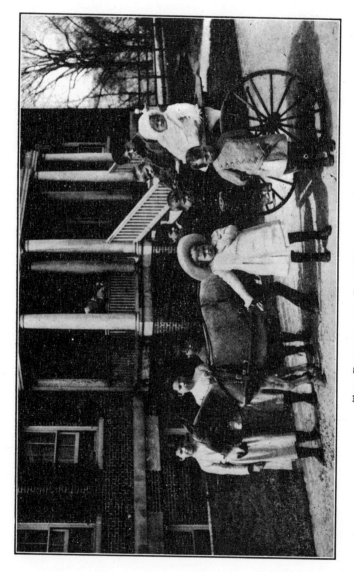

The Donkey and Cart Belong to All

tone of the school was against it. Later on, they attended school in another state where there was no sentiment against cribbing and the practice was very prevalent.

I am confident if the garden thief and the cottage vandal had been dealt with as individuals only, other similar cases would have followed, no matter what the punishment might have been. The inflicting of punishment upon a child for an offense against his fellows, by the one in authority, is by no means so effective as punishment administered by the social group injured or caused to suffer by the offense. In the latter case the moral standards of the community are defined and established by the social whole. Each individual shares in the influence and uplift of every moral judgment. The culprit also accepts his punishment with better grace, feels the force of the moral standards of the community more strongly, and is much less liable to experience feelings of personal resentment than he is when the punishment is decreed and administered by an individual.

Every enrichment of the child's life, every

new interest in play, industry or study, every increase of liberty or possession, brings new temptations. But interests and temptations, industry and freedom constitute life. They furnish the concrete situations and conditions in which moral relations arise.

G—— and K——, two boys of the Orphanage, have an unusually elaborate tree hut built some fifteen feet above the ground in a clump of chestnut trees. They wanted a waterproof roof on it. Workmen on the place were using tar paper for damp-proofing the walls of a new cottage in process of construction. The boys stole— or you may say, "carried off"—two half rolls of tar paper for use in their playhouse enterprise. At the same time they greatly needed a saw, which they also found in the contractor's outfit and appropriated. The circumstance offered an opportunity for moral instruction and moral training of which we have many in the Orphanage, and always will have as long as the children have possessions and carry on constructive play. To make things, own things, and do things is life; and life—real life—is moral. In the assembly of boys it was voted that these boys should return the stolen property, apologize to the contractor, and promise not to take anything more. They also understand that any repetition of the offense will mean a forfeit of their ownership of the house.

A——, a fourteen-year-old boy, has a dovecote which he built last year. He is raising pigeons. He needed food for them and stole a generous supply from the poultry feed room of the Orphanage. The desire to use rather than to possess was the chief motive in the theft. In the former case it was a suggestion to those in authority that children should be provided with material for their playhouse enterprises, or at least be given honest means of providing it for themselves. In the latter case opportunity to buy, or to earn by labor, food for pets was suggested and thereafter offered. It is a wise parent or teacher whose foresight is equal to these natural demands of the child's interest, and who anticipates them far enough in advance to prevent dishonest outbreaks.

Direct as well as indirect instruction in morals should be given to children. The fear of making a moral lesson or application too direct or too obvious has become a fetish with many parents and teachers, and the result often is, that no moral instruction whatever is given. The old-fashioned appeal, "Is it right?" and "Do right," are seldom heard now-a-days; and yet as long as the human mind has a conscience it is well to press these claims upon it, abstract as they are, for the response will usually be morally uplifting. In attempting to adjust methods of discipline and instruction to the caprice of the child, many parents and teachers have themselves become opportunists, relying upon devices and expedients rather than upon principles. I once knew an indulgent mother who was unable to get her young son to bed without resorting to devices, one of which was for a member of the family to impersonate a hotel proprietor, receive the boy as a guest and show him to his room.

The three following cases, in which direct instruction given in season would no doubt have served as prevention, are typical of other similar ones which have come within my experience. An undersized fourteen-year-old boy when asked

178

why he was so small for his age, told me he could not account for his lack of physical development and vigor unless it was due to smoking cigarettes, from about seven years of age until brought to the Orphanage School. He said he did not *know* the habit would injure him. He is a good boy, trustworthy and well disposed, and would no doubt never have formed the habit had he been properly instructed.

M——, now fourteen years of age, brought with her when she entered the school four years ago, a vulgar Bowery song which she immediately proceeded to teach to the other little girls. The song was brought to the office by an older girl. The child showed little knowledge of the meaning of the song when questioned about it, dropped it at once when instructed concerning it, and is now, four years later, one of the most refined girls in the school.

K——, at fifteen years of age, told me what a hard struggle he had had to break up an injurious personal habit after my first conference with the boys on the subject some two years before; also, that he had not known the practice was wrong or would work injury to him until so instructed.

Just as school nurses and settlement workers find, in thousands of homes, deplorable ignorance concerning dietary, sanitation, the care of children and the sick, resulting in ill health and a high mortality rate, so may teachers, if they inquire, find distressing ignorance among school children concerning personal habits, purity, temperance, righteous living, etc., resulting every year in a record of juvenile delinquency, vice and crime. In such cases there is need of direct instruction, and if properly given, it will go a long way toward enlightenment and prevention.

VIII
MOTIVATION AND PERSONAL TOUCH

VIII

IN all the varied experiences detailed and discussed in the foregoing chapters, there is one great principle of child training which holds a central position; namely, the importance of adequate motivation. Perhaps psychologists would call it effective stimulus. The providing of proper incentives is the largest problem in the training of children. We know that the child is capable of responding to a wide range of stimuli, and that the dynamic of growth is this power of response. If failure, poverty, misery and crime in adult society are more largely due to economic and social maladjustment than to moral causes, as some modern philanthropists claim, it is certainly to a much greater degree true that the failures and delinquencies of children are due to unfavorable environment, to lack of personal touch and methods of training, rather than to the individual qualities of the child.

Two Hundred Children

When I have attempted to attain certain definite results with children and failed, I have rarely found the chief cause of failure to lie in the children. It generally means that the motive for effort or attainment has not been adequate. The goal was too remote, appreciation of its value too slight, or there was lack of personal touch and inspiration, so that whatever was necessary to energize the full capacity of the child was wanting. The remedy would naturally be to quicken interest in the end sought.

When we first moved into our new cottage homes seven years ago, each cottage was furnished with beautiful new chinaware. The boys and girls rendered all of the service which involved the handling of china. Naturally, with so many apprentice hands, the china went to pieces at an alarming rate. To check this reckless breakage, a fine for each piece was fixed, varying according to the value of the piece but representing much less than its cost. Children charged with breakage who were not earning money worked out their fines.

This new arrangement checked the amount of

breakage, but not sufficiently to indicate proper care in handling the china or to insure valuable training and discipline for the children. The breakage went on at the average rate of about three pieces a week for each cottage. Several cottages greatly exceeded this average.

A stronger motive than money responsibility was necessary. We, therefore, fixed a maximum breakage allowance of two pieces a week for each cottage as a standard of reasonable care. If the breakage exceeded this allowance the excess was replaced with plain agateware. This new feature touched the strongest asset in the cottage system; namely, cottage pride. By carelessness on the part of those children who served in the pantry and dining room, a cottage might lose all of its beautiful china. Three of them did lose a fourth of their tableware before they became thoroughly aroused. But the effect was salutary. By the end of the first six months the total amount of breakage was reduced fifty per cent, in some cottages seventy-five per cent. An inventory and accounting is made every six months. For the past three six-month periods the average breakage per cottage has been less than one piece per week. Remarkable records have been made by certain cottages and a number of the children. It is no uncommon thing for a child to serve six months in dining room or pantry without a breakage, and the cottages that have made the best records for the past two six-month periods have broken but six and three pieces respectively.

The meaning of this little experiment in motivation, and its typical character, is the only reason for relating it in detail here. Fining the careless child for breakage was entirely an individual matter. The child broke the china, paid or worked out his fine, the breakage was replaced from the general stock, and that was the end of it. It was really nobody's affair but his own; other children of the cottage were not concerned in it. When the new feature was introduced, carelessness on the part of the individual not only meant loss to him and low grade service in pantry and dining room, but also reflected upon the social and moral standing of the whole cottage group. Breaking china became no longer merely an individual mishap; it was a social offense. The unfortunate child that tripped up and smashed a half dozen saucers stirred up the whole cottage group, and the sad consequences of his deed were brought home to him by many others who felt that it was a disgrace to be obliged to spread their table with agateware.

Of the many respects in which the cottage system of housing is superior to the congregate, none is of greater significance or more potent for moral uplift than the *esprit de corps* of the family group when once a high standard has become established. Its effect upon the individuals of the group is like that of a well-ordered family whose members feel the pressure and uplift of high moral standards, hereditary pride and social position in the community.

To relate here the many helpful ways in which the cottage spirit functions in the daily life of the Orphanage would weary the reader. From the standpoint of motivation it is a moral and social force second only to the influence of a strong personal touch. The points we wish to emphasize in the above illustration are, however, not this or that particular incentive, but the importance of finding adequate motivation for whatever is necessary to the proper training of the child; and that when failure overtakes us and the child does not respond to the stimulus offered, we should find a stronger one.

One of the most potent of all incentives in child life is the example and influence of older people whom the child respects and admires. Example and imitation always outrun instruction. This personal touch of older and wiser, but genial and companionable people, is the greatest need in child life everywhere; but its absence is more conspicuous in institution life than elsewhere, for here the proportion of adults to children is much less than in family or neighborhood life. Often the child's only point of contact with the few adults in the institution is disciplinary or governmental. The children under formal surveillance are left much to themselves. They become inexpressibly lonely although constantly in a crowd of other children.

To suppose that about all children need to make them happy are playthings and other children to play with, is a great mistake. They weary of one another much sooner than of older people. In fact, if the older associates are interesting and companionable their company is preferred to that of children.

But institution children are not the only ones that suffer from the want of friendly interest and association with older people. It is seldom that children even in their own homes receive that sympathy and co-operation from older people in either work or play, for which they deeply yearn.

At a small country resort I once saw a group of well dressed boys, apparently of good families, experimenting with a little box tortoise which they had found on one of their cross-country strolls. They wanted the creature to open its shell and put out its head. After beating it with a stick, holding it up and letting it fall to the ground, and immersing it in water, all to no effect, the poor thing being paralyzed with fear, they decided to try live coals on its back. These boys were more curious than cruel. All that most of them needed was probably just a few words on behalf of the tortoise; not a sermon, not a scientific disquisition, but simply such words as any lover of animals or sympathetic friend of dumb creatures, could speak,—awakening their interest in the quiet and lonely life of the little creature, its timid defenceless condition when overtaken by those who could move so much faster and see so much farther than it, its daily struggle to make a living, what it liked to eat and how it found its food, how easily tamed it is by kindness, etc. Scores of summer guests were lounging on the piazza smoking, reading and playing games, who could have given to these boys a small part of their time, their interest, their companionship, and thus not only have saved from torture dumb animals in the neighborhood, but what is of still greater moment, have saved the boys from the savage instincts of their own lower nature.

A boy whom I knew, who tortured a cat to death, was not cruel at heart; he was simply a young savage whose nature had never been warmed up towards cats. He had never petted a cat and listened to its gentle purr; he had never

CHRISTMAS IN PERKINS COTTAGE

CHRISTMAS IN BETHUNE COTTAGE

Motivation and Personal Touch

heard of the marvelous changes of pussy's eyes, of the delicate sensitiveness of her whiskers, of the softness, suppleness and muscular power that lie in her paws, and had never thought of her as a companion, a member of the household, doing her best to make the home brighter and happier.

Thousands of offenses designated by the law as misdemeanors or crimes, and many a fiendish piece of deviltry not put down in law books, are committed during the long vacation each year because a great army of boys is turned loose on the community with nothing to do. Their time is not motived.

The public playground movement is good as far as it goes, but a fourteen-year-old boy is not satisfied with playing all of the time. He wants some work. His nature calls for some kind of constructive industry, such as a farm, a garden, a work bench, a flower bed, a store, a shop, or the care of stock, offers. It is a serious social and economic blunder to leave boys to their own resources without suggestion or aid, while vacant lots lie idle, second hand nails are rusting

in old decaying store boxes, and many an old
saw, hammer, spade and rake are hanging on
pegs in cellars and woodsheds.

All that is required is that the grown-up people
in each community should feel responsible for
awakening wholesome interests and useful activities in the boys who are turned loose to wander
aimlessly about. The mere presence and participation of an older person whom the children
like will frequently furnish all the motive needed
to produce energetic work or spirited play.

Writers on the care of dependent and delinquent
children have dwelt long and earnestly upon the
various means of providing for them. Institutional care, legal adoption, the placing out and
boarding out systems, cottage and congregate
plans of housing, urban and rural environments,
etc., have all had their turn in the discussion.
The time has come to shift the emphasis from
houses and lands to a more vital center of educative force in the life of the child; namely, to the
personality of teacher, foster parent or companion.

Some time ago I sent out the following card
from the Orphanage:

Motivation and Personal Touch

"The problem that confronts this institution is the education of two hundred orphan children. Our purpose is to give the best education possible for character and efficiency. We are seeking the opinions of several thousand representative men and women. You can assist us greatly in determining the proper distribution of educative effort and emphasis by estimating the relative values of the factors enumerated below: first, as they functioned in your own early life; second, as you would value them in an ideal scheme of education. The list is not exhaustive; heredity is purposely omitted. A single one of the list might in individual cases function so largely as to exclude one or more of the others. Please estimate in the second column, however, with the understanding that all shall function and without special reference to the training of orphan children. Each column should foot up one hundred per cent as indicated.

	Estimate in Your Life	Ideal Values
1. The home and its surroundings, not including persons.............	..	..
2. Personal influence of parents, teachers and associates	..	..
3. Regular school instruction.........	..	..
4. Direct moral instruction, correction and punishment	..	..
5. Religious instruction and training..	..	..
6. School instruction in manual training	..	..
7. Training in home duties and responsibilities	..	..
8. Reading of books outside of school.	..	..
Total 100%		100%

Two Hundred Children

From the cards already returned, a number of which have been filled out by leading educators, it is clear that the second item in the list holds a high place in the estimation of all who have weighed the factors enumerated. The average for this one factor is about thirty per cent, or nearly one-third of the total estimate for all the factors.

There is little doubt that this estimate would remain constant and close to the above average if the number of cards returned should run up into the thousands. From the standpoint of character and efficiency, environment, housing, formal instruction, etc., are not half so important as teachers and associates.

Of all the working forces which make or mar the child's future well-being, the personality of those in close touch with him far outranks every other influence.

If the placing out system has any great advantage over institutional care, it will be on account of the superior personalities with whom the child comes in contact, or a larger share in association with these personalities than is

Motivation and Personal Touch

possible in the institution. On the other hand, if the institution is so managed that the children come into intimate relations with adult characters who are strong, sympathetic, intellectually alert, and socially, morally and spiritually uplifting, it ceases to be a mere abiding place where the creature comforts only are provided, and becomes a school home from which the children go forth better prepared to make their own way in the world than are most of those set adrift from their parental homes at the same age.

Wherever the dependent child is, whether in a foster home or an institution, he will make but little headway if left to himself and his environment. He must have the society, or better, comradeship, as well as the instruction of older people who are interested in him. He must be known and trained according to his personal and individual characteristics and not merely by a name or number. Institutionalism, whether it exists in the form of congregate housing or the cottage system—for it may exist in either— is opposed to this recognition of the child's individuality. It is rote, routine and dead-

levelism. It is law, coercion and suppression. It
is praying by rote, singing by rote, repeating por-
tions of the Bible by rote. It is walking in silent
rows, eating in silent rows, sleeping in silent
rows. It is religion without personality, discipline
without individuality, and play without initiative.

But it is as easy to find defects in family training
as in institutional. The attempt to escape their
God-given responsibility by many parents now-
a-days is the chief cause for juvenile delinquency,
of well-filled protectories, reformatories and so-
called "industrial schools."

One parent in a neighboring state gained considerable notoriety through the daily press a
short time ago by claiming a new idea for re-
lieving parents of the burden of personally
looking after and associating with their children.
The plan proposed was the building of a bungalow
near the parental home in which the six boys
of the family, all under sixteen years of age,
were to live. They were not to enter their
parents' home except on invitation. Such a
scheme implies that the home cannot or will not
adapt itself to the needs of the natural boy,

or else the natural boy must necessarily make himself a nuisance in the ordinary home. Both of these implications may be true, and probably they are true in many of even our well-to-do homes, where the parents are willing to give their children everything except their greatest gift, and that which the child most needs—themselves.

The deepest meaning of home is associated with children; with their freedom and spontaneity, their sunshine and shadows, their joys and tears; with the roistering, rollicking exuberance of boys, and the gentler play-loving nature of girls. It is these things that enrich and endear home life to both parents and children, taking away from it the boarding-house atmosphere. Children can receive from their parents the heritage of culture to which they are entitled only by living with them. The best that has come to parents and teachers through heredity, education and experience, can be passed on to their children, not by formal instruction, but through comradeship and intimate association with them in all of the relations and interests which enlarge and enrich home life.

Two Hundred Children

The most precious thing you can give a child is yourself. Wise parents will enter into the games and pastimes of their children, will swim and skate and coast with them, will read and stroll and play games with them, will plan and build and sympathize with them in their struggles, in their failures, and in the training of their pets.

But all this means the spending of a great deal of time with one's children. Outside of the time required for providing the means of support for the family, I know of no better way, however, in which parents may employ their time. It is not only the child that is benefited; it builds character in the parents as well, and it keeps them young. The period of childhood is all too short to those parents who enter into the spirit of child life. The time will come too soon when the absence of dolls, toy dogs and tin soldiers, scattered about the room—even the family sitting room—and the barrenness of the corners and closets where bats and balls, rackets and mitts were wont to lie, will bring loneliness to the heart and moisture to the eyes. Our boys and girls are children but once, and childhood days are short.

Motivation and Personal Touch

In both the placing out system and in institutional care of children, too little attention has been paid to the personality of those responsible for them. Those who find homes for children frequently exhibit photographs of the home and its environment, pictures of the child driving a pony cart followed by a pet dog, etc. A photograph of the foster parents accompanied with a character sketch and a report of hours a day or week spent with the child would be worth more than a whole herd of ponies and dogs, dear as these pets may be to the ordinary child. It really makes little difference whether the foster home is a beautiful house surrounded by lawns and gardens with shade trees and piazzas, serpentine walks and rose bushes, or just a plain four-walled structure at the cross-roads of a treeless prairie where the monotonous expanse of broad-acred grain fields meet. Love of home, sweetness and light, and the development of character, may go with either, provided, the personalities are there in which these qualities live and grow. Daily association and companionship with a strong, sympathetic and lovable character is a

Two Hundred Children

brief but comprehensive description of a happy condition of child life. The child that has such a heritage for his early years needs little else, and he that lacks it will be little the better off for anything else he may have.

IX
RELIGIOUS INSTRUCTION AND TRAINING

IX

THE child is a physical, intellectual, moral and religious being. A system of education which neglects any part of his fourfold nature is incomplete. Instruction in religion should be definite and positive. In our zeal for liberty of conscience we have gone so far that even parents sometimes feel that they are infringing upon the personal rights of their children when they enter this field of instruction. To let the child grow up a pagan and then choose for himself is the custom of many parents in this country today.

The same neglect and lack of faith characterizes too much of our social and philanthropic endeavor. We are prone to account for human depravity on economic rather than on moral grounds, and to seek amelioration of bad social conditions through legislation or makeshift betterments rather than by the moral quickening and cleansing of the soul through the religious appeal. Any effort that makes for civic righteousness should be welcomed through whatever means it may come. But a positive, working faith in God is the only true and adequate source of relief. Other foundation can no man lay.

In a recent address Dr. Thomas Darlington, President of the New York Board of Health, said, "There are one hundred and eighty-six laws in the Sanitary Code of New York City, and every one of them is founded on the commandment: 'Love thy neighbor as thyself.' If that commandment were fully observed, not one of these laws would be broken."—And, we may add, "would be needed."

It is unfortunate for our children that church and state cannot co-operate in their religious education, for education without religion is seriously defective. With such diversity of religious views and tenets as were held by the founders of the Nation and by the inpouring throngs of immigrants for the past century, it is difficult to see how any form of co-operation providing for religious education could have been effected. The

Religious Instruction and Training

need of such co-operation or of the state assuming any responsibility for instruction in religion was not apparent when the thin edge of the wedge first began to push the church and the school apart. The church had dominated learning and the schools for so many centuries that no one imagined that they could live apart. Schools without religious instruction for the children would have outraged the conscience and zeal for piety of our forebears.

In the chapter on moral training we have already called attention to the secularization of the common school curriculum. This movement followed the decline of the Puritan spirit after the Revolution. The early school readers were religious as well as secular books. In the Abecedarian, the alphabet and ab, eb, ib, columns were followed by the Credo and Paternoster; later, the Ave Maria and, soon after the thirteenth century, the Benedicite and Gratias were included. The forty-fifth canon of the Council of Mainz, in the year eight hundred and thirteen, decreed that children should be taught the "fidem catholicam et orationem dominicam." This established the curriculum of elementary education and determined its subject matter. From Charles the Great to Luther, no other material than the above appeared in school readers. The Enschedé Abecedarium, which has been claimed as the first specimen of printing with type, contained the alphabet, the Paternoster, the Ave Maria, the Credo, and two prayers. This was the elementary book of the Roman Catholic Church.

The early primers of the Reformation were not only school books but manuals of church service. In fact the German word for primer—Fibel—which first appeared in a "Kölner Glossar" in 1419, signifies a little Bible. Henry VIII issued proclamations and injunctions against the printing of unauthorized primers in his endeavor to keep his people true to Catholicism. A little later and after his "change of heart," he used the same weapon for fighting the Pope and issued his Reform Primer, designed to teach his people the true doctrine.

Thus did alphabet and Creed become united in one book, and Catholic and Protestant primers included both religious and secular matter. Lu-

Religious Instruction and Training

ther's Child's Primer contained the Lord's Prayer, the Commandments, the Creed and the Catechism. The New England Primer, the most popular text-book in America during the colonial period, was a church book, although it contained secular matter along with the catechism.

Of the change to secular matter in the composition of school readers which followed the Revolution, George H. Martin in "Evolution of Massachusetts Public School System" says, "Its influence was deep and abiding. The substitution of the selfish and sordid aphorisms of Franklin for the Proverbs of Solomon and the divine precepts of the Sermon on the Mount; the declarations of Webster and Pitt for the lofty patriotism of Moses and Isaiah; the feeble reasoning of Mrs. Barbauld and Hannah More for the compact logic of Paul's Epistles; the tinsel glitter of Byron for the inspiring devotion of David, and the showy scene-painting in the narrations of Scott for the simplicity of the Gospel story of the life of Christ— such a substitution could not take place without modifying subtly but surely all the life currents of the community."

Two Hundred Children

The loss was not only to religion but to morality, for the natural starting point and the surest foundation for moral instruction is the religious instinct. To attempt to rear a moral structure in the child soul on any other foundation is an uncertain, if not, indeed, an impossible task. The religious sense gets in its work much earlier than the moral. It begins before the moral feelings awaken. Under normal family conditions the little child learns to pray long before he learns to speak the truth. In fact, it is a question whether as a child he will acquire the moral habit of honesty without a sense of responsibility to a Divine Being. To demand moral training in any large measure of our public schools, in which instruction in religion and the use of the Bible are forbidden, is unreasonable and unfair. To go blindly ahead with a great system of public education while making no provision whatever for religious instruction upon which to support a moral structure of conscience and character, is to maintain an enterprise at great cost with no assurance of safe returns on the investment.

It is a significant fact that the growth of re-

Religious Instruction and Training

ligious denominationalism, the development of
the Sunday School and the secularization of the
public school curriculum were contemporary and
parallel movements in the progress of education
in this country. No doubt many who have
watched and welcomed the gradual widening of
the breach between the church and the public
schools have felt that the home and the Sunday
School should make good to the child the loss
he has suffered by this separation.

As the material for religious instruction—
mostly Bible stories and quotations—gradually
disappeared from the school readers, the Sunday
School developed and its special literature increased. But the secular school, with its paid
teachers, competitive systems, text-book enterprises, normal schools, and state support, soon left
far behind the Sunday School with its unsalaried
and untrained teachers and officers, its voluntary
attendance, and its antiquated methods of instruction. From the standpoint of trained teachers, a suitable course of study and rational methods of instruction, the Sunday School has not advanced much beyond where it was when secular

and religious instruction parted company nearly a century ago. So slipshod and desultory is much of our Sunday School teaching that the disparagement is sometimes expressed by the conundrum, "When is a school not a school?"—"When it is a Sunday School." I verily believe that the only thing that keeps the Sunday School going at all and accomplishing so much with the small proportion of children who attend, is the fact that the subject matter of its curriculum is the inspired Word. For if similar loose and dilettante organization and methods were followed in teaching the branches of our common school curriculum, the whole school enterprise would speedily go to pieces.

Not much can be said in praise of many of the homes of our country as centers of religious instruction. Here again the children have suffered inestimable loss and been doomed to grow up with no religious instruction because the parents held diverse views or no definite convictions at all, and did not even give the Sunday School or church a chance at enlightening their children.

Two boys, one twelve and the other fourteen

Religious Instruction and Training

years of age, were admitted to this Orphanage a
week ago. They were born and have always lived
in New York City. The mother was formerly a
Catholic, but after her marriage got out of touch
with the church. The father was a Protestant.
The children were baptized in a Protestant church.
The boys have always attended school in New
York City and are further along in the course than
the average boys of their age who enter the Orphanage. The older boy is bright and intelligent and ready for eighth grade work. He is in
almost absolute ignorance of the Bible, can remember attending church service but twice in all
his life, and but once going to a Catholic Sunday
School. The boys know almost nothing of the
Bible, not even the story of Joseph. They say
there was no Bible in their home. Their father,
who was a hotel waiter, was absent every Sunday
until he contracted the illness from which he died.
The boys received no religious instruction from
their mother.

Here then are two bright, capable boys in whose
lives religious instruction has had no place. They
are the product of a non-religious home and school

training, and are typical of thousands of other children growing up in unenlightened homes of our land even where no such difference of religious views between parents, as in this case, exists. Such children are deprived of their sacred birthright. In some manner, not yet clear perhaps to anyone, our great public educational system must rescue from ignorance these unfortunates—must meet this need. The equipment and organization—the public school plant—will not be worked to its capacity until it serves in this field also.

Our schools are not yet Godless, as some critics of our public school system charge. There are too many consecrated teachers on the rolls to justify the claim. But it is hardly fair to expect teachers whose lips are sealed to religious instruction to save the day against a public policy which is indifferent. The situation cannot long remain where it is. It will grow better by a change of public sentiment with respect to this defect in elementary education, or worse by further elimination of the religious interest. The breeding-in process of supplying teachers is gradually working in this latter direction. The pupils of today become the teachers of tomorrow, and with a constantly diminishing religious element in the curriculum, the teaching force is certain to become less and less of a religious factor in its official capacity. Is it too much to expect that a national religious consciousness will yet arise, assert itself, and restore to the children of the Nation their lost birthright? Does the organization of a National Religious Educational Association indicate such a movement?

Society is gradually assuming increased responsibility for the care and education of children. The compulsory attendance law, the truant officer, protection from premature employment, the school doctor and nurse, represent this movement. Is it wise to assume so much care for the child's physical wellbeing and minister not at all to this higher craving of the soul? Of course the state cannot definitely prescribe the content of religious instruction, but it can lend its superb equipment, its plant, buildings, apparatus, appliances, etc., to a work which is as essential to its self preservation as any other interest which this great investment serves.

Two Hundred Children

The Sunday School work, imperfect as it is, is nevertheless enlarging and improving. Even a silent endorsement on the part of the state by offering its splendid public education plant for religious teaching, would give a tremendous impetus to such instruction. As the buildings are quiet and empty—a dead investment—about half of the time when it would be practicable to use them, such instruction need not interfere in the least with the hours of secular teaching. Everywhere the people look upon the public school buildings as theirs, and they covet earnestly the instruction offered in the schools. Here are class rooms, furniture, blackboards, maps, musical instruments, etc. Many a good secular school teacher would teach religion if such an opportunity were offered, and thousands of parents would take advantage of such instruction for their children, who could attend in plain, every-day school clothes. Parents could have their children instructed in harmony with their own religious faith or preference. The plant is ample for all the demands of diverse views, and denominational zeal need not be hampered or suppressed.

Religious Instruction and Training

This would also infuse a measure of pedagogical procedure into Sunday School teaching in which element at present it is woefully lacking.

The conditions in most of our churches for Sunday School instruction are wretched. Many classes recite in one room, there are but few or no modern appliances and aids to instruction, which with the bedlam of many voices and consequent disorder and lack of attention, renders futile most of the energy expended.

It is a great privilege, in the schoolroom where secular subjects are taught, to feel absolutely free to present religious truth, or appeal to the religious motives, when incident or occasion naturally suggests them. In the educational work of this Orphanage no sharp separation of sacred and secular truth is necessary. The child learns the truths of religion along with the other matter of the curriculum. Thus, in presenting the story of Esther in a Sunday School lesson, it was observed that the children were very much interested in the various situations and characters. But it could receive only a touch-and-go treatment in the brief time allotted to such a lesson. During the fol-

lowing week the English period of the four upper
grades of the Orphanage school was devoted to the
story for a more detailed and thorough study than
was possible in the Sunday School. The children
studied it as literature and history, and also in its
moral, political, and religious bearings upon life.
With the colored slides and a stereopticon, an
evening was devoted to it. Finally, each child
wrote his own version of the entire story and drew
a sketch of the critical moment when the golden
scepter was extended by Ahasuerus or the decree
presented to Esther by Mordecai. Thus, with a
free curriculum—free as regards religious subject
matter and instruction—the purest, the truest, the
most life giving literature of all the ages is at the
service of teachers and pupils. In this case, as in
countless similar ones that arise, they were able
to do what the ordinary Sunday School could not
do because of having no hold on the pupils, and
what the public school would not be allowed to
do because such a study of the Bible would violate
the religious neutrality of the curriculum. These
boys and girls were able to stay with this story
long enough to extract out of it all there was in it

for them, of English, of literature, of history, art and religion.

The life stories of the great Bible characters are treated in a similar manner; that is, the weekday school follows up and completes what the Sunday School is able only to begin. In this way the children are living every week with these great personalities, the examples and leaders of our race. To exclude from our everyday elementary school instruction the literature of the Bible is to withhold from the children of the nation the knowledge and inspiration of the greatest educational classics in existence.

Religious instruction should be as clear and intelligent to the child as instruction in geography or history. The mechanical or rote memorizing of so many songs and psalms or chapters adapted to adult saints, or the monotonous mumbling of prayers which carry no meaning to the child mind should have no place. But much of the Bible truth should be memorized when it is studied, explained and understood. A few well chosen quotations will usually fix the great principles or striking qualities of strength or weakness in the characters studied. Thus:

13 And Samuel came to Saul: and Saul said unto him, Blessed be thou of the LORD: I have performed the commandment of the LORD.

14 And Samuel said, What meaneth then this bleating of the sheep in mine ears, and the lowing of the oxen which I hear?

And Saul said, They have brought them from the Amalekites: for the people spared the best of the sheep and of the oxen to sacrifice unto the LORD thy God; and the rest we have utterly destroyed.

And Samuel said, Hath the LORD as great delight in burnt offerings and sacrifices, as in obeying the voice of the LORD? Behold, to obey is better than sacrifice, and to hearken than the fat of rams.

About the time that this incident was being studied one of our boys left the Orphanage grounds without permission and entered the cherry orchard of a neighbor, and picked several quarts of cherries. When caught in the act, his plea was that he was picking cherries "for my cottage mother." The application of the text was readily made.

The quotations which have been selected for memorizing after a study of any given character or incident has been made are often called for as a part of daily chapel exercises. Thus:

"Quote the classical expression for personal attachment."

The children respond with Ruth's words to Naomi:

16 And Ruth said, Intreat me not to leave thee, or to return from following after thee: for whither thou goest, I will go; and where thou lodgest, I will lodge: thy people shall be my people, and thy God my God:

17 Where thou diest, will I die, and there will I be buried: the LORD do so to me, and more also, if aught but death part thee and me.

The classical expression for patriotic devotion:

By the rivers of Babylon, there we sat down, yea we wept, when we remembered Zion.

2 We hanged our harps upon the willows in the midst thereof.

3 For there they that carried us away captive required of us a song; and they that wasted us required of us mirth, saying, Sing us one of the songs of Zion.

4 How shall we sing the LORD's song in a strange land?

5 If I forget thee, O Jerusalem, let my right hand forget her cunning.

6 If I do not remember thee, let my tongue cleave

Two Hundred Children

to the roof of my mouth; if I prefer not Jerusalem above my chief joy.

For peace:

4 And he shall judge among the nations, and shall rebuke many people: and they shall beat their swords into plowshares, and their spears into pruninghooks: nation shall not lift up sword against nation, neither shall they learn war any more.

For God's estimate of a human soul:

Thus saith the LORD, The heaven is my throne, and the earth is my footstool: where is the house that ye build unto me? and where is the place of my rest?

2 For all those things hath mine hand made, and all those things have been, saith the LORD: but to this man will I look, even to him that is poor and of a contrite spirit, and trembleth at my word.

For Peter's conversion to the universal Fatherhood of God:

34 Then Peter opened his mouth, and said, Of a truth I perceive that God is no respecter of persons:

35 But in every nation he that feareth him, and worketh righteousness, is accepted with him.

Of kingly humility:

7 And now, O LORD my God, thou hast made thy servant king instead of David my father: and I am

but a little child: I know not how to go out or come in.

8 And thy servant is in the midst of thy people which thou hast chosen, a great people, that cannot be numbered nor counted for multitude.

9 Give therefore thy servant an understanding heart to judge thy people, that I may discern between good and bad: for who is able to judge this thy so great a people?

The classic parable for illustrating the Father's love in the story of the prodigal son is memorized. Also quotations designated after the following manner.

The influence of Paul's preaching upon Felix:

25 And as he reasoned of righteousness, temperance, and judgment to come, Felix trembled, and answered, Go thy way for this time; when I have a convenient season, I will call for thee.

Paul's energy and singleness of purpose:

13 Brethren, I count not myself to have apprehended: but this one thing I do, forgetting those things which are behind, and reaching forth unto those things which are before,

14 I press toward the mark for the prize of the high calling of God in Christ Jesus.

221

Two Hundred Children

Paul's final words:

6 For I am now ready to be offered, and the time of my departure is at hand.

7 I have fought a good fight, I have finished my course, I have kept the faith:

8 Henceforth there is laid up for me a crown of righteousness, which the Lord, the righteous judge, shall give me at that day: and not to me only, but unto all them also that love his appearing.

The prayers of the Pharisee and the publican:

10 Two men went up into the temple to pray; the one a Pharisee, and the other a publican.

11 The Pharisee stood and prayed thus with himself, God, I thank thee, that I am not as other men are, extortioners, unjust, adulterers, or even as this publican.

12 I fast twice in the week, I give tithes of all that I possess.

13 And the publican, standing afar off, would not lift up so much as his eyes unto heaven, but smote upon his breast, saying, God be merciful to me a sinner.

14 I tell you, this man went down to his house justified rather than the other: for every one that exalteth himself shall be abased; and he that humbleth himself shall be exalted.

The announcement of the birth of Christ to the shepherds ending with:

Religious Instruction and Training

14 Glory to God in the highest, and on earth peace, good will toward men.

Christ's conversation with the woman of Samaria at the historic well, leading up to the sublime utterance:

24 God is a Spirit: and they that worship him must worship him in spirit and in truth.

The lawyer's question and answer in the parable of the Good Samaritan—Luke X, 25–37.

The conclusion of the whole matter:

8 He hath shewed thee, O man, what is good; and what doth the LORD require of thee, but to do justly, and to love mercy, and to walk humbly with thy God?

13 Let us hear the conclusion of the whole matter: Fear God, and keep his commandments: for this is the whole duty of man.

14 For God shall bring every work into judgment, with every secret thing, whether it be good, or whether it be evil.

Such classification and memorizing of Bible truth, always in connection with the concrete and detailed study of characters and incidents, is a part of the weekly program in the work of this Orphanage. It is what we mean when we say that instruction in religion should appeal to the child's intelligence and should be rich in thought content. No other treasury of truth in any form anywhere can compare in richness, beauty and strength with the legacy that has been passed on to us in the life story, the words and deeds of the great Bible characters—Abraham, Joseph, Moses, David, Daniel, the Christ, Peter, Paul and others. It is the literature of power through which the most practical as well as the purest and deepest truths of life find their way into the mind and heart of the child. Not to know this literature in childhood is to lose the most valuable heritage of our spiritual birthright. With such a foundation and background, instruction in morals and moral training may go forward in a sound and sure way.

We must distinguish between instruction in religion and religious living. Religion itself—the real thing—is extremely elusive when we attempt to define it, or to teach it by direct means. Religion manifests itself in acts of worship, in forms and ceremonies, in literature, art and music. But these are not religion. The essence of religion is the consciousness of a divine personality to whom we are related through a sense of sin, through fear, faith, trust and love.

Religious training is not something put on; it should develop naturally, starting with the native instincts of fear, faith and love. Reverence for the supernatural is present in every child. Man *is* a religious being; he does not become such. The mistake has too often been made of looking upon religion as something above natural human experience and beyond or outside of everyday affairs.

While these words were being written, a fourteen-year-old boy entered my office and asked if he might quit school and go to work. He has attended the High School for one year, is a bright, capable boy, but desultory in both academic and industrial work. I endeavored to show him what a serious decision he was about to make, what a far-reaching influence it was certain to have on his future life, and how important it was that he should consider the matter carefully before making up his mind. I also tried to ascertain just what had brought about his present state of mind with respect to further school attendance. The matter was then

Two Hundred Children

left, with the understanding that he is to carefully reconsider the question, carry it up to a Higher Wisdom in prayer for guidance, and then come to me again for further conference. It is extremely important that this child, as every other child, or man, should pause long enough before each important decision or choice in life to seek guidance from a higher source than human agency can offer.

The most consequential and far-reaching decisions in life must be made and are made during the years of immaturity and inexperience. This arrangement would seem to indicate that the All-wise Father intended that his children should consult Him in settling questions upon which momentous and lifelong issues depend. Children while still children may be taught through their own experience to take God into account in settling these great questions. They should be urged, in every puzzling situation of life, to enquire of Him who knows and to plead for the touch of the Hand which unerringly guides. What better habit can any one form? This is simply applied religion—or religion at work in everyday life.

Religious Instruction and Training

Religion without morality is mere form, if not hypocrisy. Morality without religion—in child life at least—is cold, empty, and uncertain, wanting in grip and anchorage. Why is it that in seeking to obtain a confession of wrong-doing from a guilty child, an appeal based upon religious grounds will succeed after every possible approach on moral grounds has failed? Again and again I have attempted to lead children into a proper attitude toward their wrong deeds by presenting the moral bearings of the case, and failed. The wrongdoer seems much better able to nerve himself up to withstand an appeal based upon moral grounds. He knows the deed he has committed is wrong and expects to face the consequences. But shift his sense of responsibility, or accountability, to a Divine Personality instead of an abstract principle and he is almost sure to mellow at once, to confess his wrong, and to come into such moral relation to his deed as may be necessary to establish the basis for a new start.

Religious motives, like the play instinct, the constructive and economic interest, etc., should function in the daily life of the child. To receive religious and moral instruction and fail to apply the lessons in practical experience is "Like unto a man beholding his natural face in a glass, for he beholdeth himself and goeth his way and straightway forgetteth what manner of man he was." Honesty, industry, economy, protection of property, the square deal, fair play, kindness, helpfulness, mutual service, faith in God and the consciousness of Divine support, guidance and protection, must function in the experience of the child if they are to have any significance whatever beyond mere form and an empty, passive, intellectual assent.

In the training of children we appeal frequently to the child's play or industrial interests, to his literary or artistic appreciation, to his sense of right and wrong. Why should we not as readily appeal to his religious instinct and interest? It is just as true to say he is religious as to say he is playful or constructive, or that he loves color.

If the essential elements of religion are faith, hope and love, the little child enters more naturally into religious experience than the adult, for he possesses these qualities in greater proportion

Religious Instruction and Training

to the counter qualities of doubt, despair and hate.
A wise religious training will keep alive and active
these cardinal virtues of religion while at the same
time developing through experience and observation such a necessary proportion of doubts and
fears, of distrust of evildoers and their methods,
in a word, of worldly wisdom, and practical knowledge of life, as is sufficient to safeguard the child
against those who would exploit his innocence.

SUPPLEMENT
THE DIARY OF A DAY

THE DIARY OF A DAY

PERHAPS the truest description of how children "live and learn" in their own homes can be written by themselves. The following are copies of twenty-five school papers written by the boys and girls of different ages, of this Orphanage, on the subject, "How I Spent Last Saturday." They present in detail the Saturday life and experiences of the children and illustrate many points discussed in the foregoing chapters. The place of home-making industries in the child's life, the range of occupation and recreation, individual initiative, freedom from surveillance, (any boy may go a-fishing if he can swim,) the economic interest, mutual service, ownership and care of pets, etc., all appear in the doings of a day.

In the morning I had to put the breakfast on the table. After breakfast my work was to help in the kitchen until noon, then I helped get dinner. After dinner I washed the dishes and when I had finished that I took a bath. After bathing I made arrangements with William Kidd to go fishing and we went to Harriman's Dock, but we did not catch any fish. We then went to the Amackassin Dock. While there we learned how to catch eels in a different way than the way we had always caught them.

When we returned from fishing I played ball until our supper bell rang and I had to go in and put supper on the table for the boys in our cottage. After supper I washed the dishes quickly and then went out and played ball until the curfew rang. We then all came into the library to read books or magazines. At half past eight we went to bed.

Lawrence Welch

15 years
Rogers Cottage

In the early morning I dressed, went down stairs and moulded the bread I had made the night before into pans, after which I had my breakfast.

About seven o'clock I went over to the Administration Building and cleaned the offices, the Board room and the teachers' room. I finished this cleaning about eleven o'clock, went home and cleaned my own room. It was then time for dinner. After dinner I read to a few of the little children from a book called "Miss Minchin." About two o'clock a few of the girls and myself who sing in the choir went to rehearse some music at the M. E. Church in Yonkers. We arrived home at half past four and I soon became very much interested in watching a ball game played by our boys. At half past five I prepared supper. After supper I

The Diary of a Day

worked six arithmetic problems, after which I played games with the girls until it was time for me to go to bed.

Alva Stewart

16 years

Perkins Cottage

All the forenoon I worked in the kitchen and helped to put on the food for dinner. At one thirty I helped in the kitchen again until about two o'clock. From two to four o'clock I picked dandelions and earned six cents. I then went up to my pigeon house and fixed it. Then I helped to put the food on the table for supper. After supper I fed and watered my pigeons and read "With Lee in Virginia."

Frank Ahlheim

13 years

Graham Cottage

Saturday morning I worked until nine o'clock sweeping, dusting and polishing the hall. I went out of doors to play till half past ten, then I came in and got ready for sewing class. I stayed till twelve o'clock. During that time I worked on a hem stitched handkerchief and practiced button-hole work and chain stitch. In the afternoon I went out doors again and played on the lawn with my doll. I soon got tired of holding my doll and so played baseball a little while, then I went down to the barn for chicken feed.

Helen Kurz

11 years

Hamilton Cottage

Two Hundred Children

Saturday morning at six o'clock I was called to help get breakfast ready. After breakfast was on the table I rang the bell. After breakfast I went up stairs to make my bed. Then I went down stairs in the kitchen and washed the breakfast dishes quite early, and then helped to make some things for dinner. There was a little time left so I scrubbed the floor. I finished that about half past eleven. Then I put the food on the tables for dinner and rang the bell.

After dinner I washed the dishes and did my other work. I fixed the fire and went out to play. The Graham boys and the Satterlee boys played ball. We played three innings. About four o'clock the large boys came out to play and then they picked sides. I played till five o'clock and then rang the bell for the boys. I helped get supper on the tables and rang the bell. After supper I did my regular work and cooked the cereal for breakfast, fixed the fire and went out to play.

William Miner

13 years

Satterlee Cottage

I swept, dusted and cleaned the front hall which kept me at work until ten o'clock, then I scrubbed the front porch. All together it was about eleven thirty when I was through with my work. Then I read until dinner time from a book called "The Lost Treasure Cave."

After dinner Miss T—— wanted a boy to do some odd jobs for her and I was told to do them. I dug up

The Diary of a Day

some soil, planted some dahlias and sodded around the front porch and walks. About four o'clock I finished. Being pretty dirty I took a bath and then read until supper time. After supper I played games such as tag and other things.

Harold Paul

13 years

Rogers Cottage

After breakfast I made my bed and swept the laundry. Then I went to sewing class and there I worked on my apron. At eleven o'clock I went home and sat on the lawn with a little kitten in my lap. Then I ate my dinner.

After dinner I helped the little children get ready to go out. After this I went to the Church with some other girls to practice with the choir. When I came home I changed my clothes, ate my supper and cleaned the dining room. Then I went out and ran all over the lawn until my bed time.

Florence Schoen

12 years

Perkins Cottage

I spent most of my time in the cottage until 9 o'clock. I worked in one of the small bedrooms. After I was dismissed from the cottage I had a game of ball, then after that I went and picked two pails of dandelions. Then our dinner bell rang. After dinner another boy and I washed the dishes that were in the

Two Hundred Children

pantry. Then I picked five pailsful of dandelions. I put them together and took them to Mr. R——. He gave me fifteen cents for them. I asked Mr. B—— for work and helped him pick up papers around the grounds. I then swept the Warburton gutters and I helped distribute parsnips and onions to the cottages. I saved the money that I received.

George Wolf

13 years

Bethune Cottage

In the morning I cleaned the dining room and the silver. At eleven o'clock I went to sewing class and sewed on my doily. Then I traced some butterflies for the girls to buttonhole while Miss S—— is on her vacation.

At twelve o'clock I went home to my dinner. After dinner I swept the dining room floor and helped carry water down to our chicken coop.

In the afternoon I picked a large bunch of violets, after which I took a walk around the grounds. Then I went to get some wild flowers.

Two friends came to play with us. We took them over to the toboggan slide where we had great sport. After the friends went home I came over to the house and read a book called "The Bandmaster." After supper I read in the library until bed time.

Mary Kohout

12 years

Perkins Cottage

The Diary of a Day

Saturday before breakfast I swept the basement and scoured the sink. Then I washed, cleaned my teeth well and went into the dining room where I ate my breakfast. After breakfast I made my bed, after which I went down stairs and emptied the dirt barrel and burned the rubbish. When I had put my barrel away and had finished my work in the cottage I put up a bird house in the bushes next to our cottage. I softened up and made level the dirt on our lawn. After dinner I went out into the pantry and helped wash the dishes. When the dishes were finished I had to go out and work again on the lawn with my pickax and shovel. I worked there until Mr. R—— asked for the horse that was carrying dirt to our cottage, then I was allowed to go out and play ball. When the game was finished I went into the cottage and read until the bell rang for supper. After supper I went out and played tag until the curfew rang when I came in and went to bed.

Albert Roche

12 years

Satterlee Cottage

On Saturday all the boys in our cottage have to work in the morning. After I had finished my regular work which consists in cleaning the matron's room, I waxed the library floor and then went to dinner. After dinner I polished the kitchen stove and helped the kitchen boy. Then I worked in the basement. My work for the day being done I went down in the woods to see how many wild flowers I could find. I found the blue violet, white violet, the May flower, wild geranium and another flower which I did not know. I then went out on the grounds and watched a game of ball between the boys of two of our cottages. Some of the older boys came along and picked sides for another game. I was chosen but happened to be on the losing side. I then went to supper.

After supper I played ball until the curfew rang.

Harry Kohout
14 years
Rogers Cottage

Saturday morning I got up early, prepared the yellow meal and made milk toast for breakfast. In the morning I made a loaf cake, baked bread and made rolls, also stewed fruit, made two loaves of brown bread, prepared the baked beans for the oven and got dinner ready which consisted of creamed codfish, mashed potatoes and bread pudding. In the afternoon Janet and I went to Yonkers to see Tessie. In the evening I played Parchesi and indoor baseball, after which I studied my Sunday School lesson.

Amelia Wingerter
15 years
Perkins Cottage

Before breakfast I dressed, washed and went down stairs. Then Harry Kohout asked me to help him with the library work. I helped him carry out the chairs. After this was done, I put the chairs back on the carpet

The Diary of a Day

in their right places. I also dusted the table and put
the books on. Then I dusted the windows and the
baseboards. Soon the library work was done. While
I was putting the magazines and "Boys' Worlds" in
order, I saw a nice story called "Where the Sea Flag
Floats." I had time to read one chapter before the
bell rang.

After breakfast I did my work with Henry Burkle,
which was to sweep, polish, dust and put the beds in
order. After I had my bath I went down to the
basement to skate. Then I took off my skates and
went up stairs to read the rest of the story which I
had begun before breakfast. I finished that and then
drew pictures. The first picture I drew was of a battle
between Spain and America. Then the bell rang and
I ate my dinner. After dinner I asked my cottage
mother for my money to buy oranges. I bought some
oranges and then went to the barn to see Rex harness
the horses. He asked me if I would hold Harry, the
horse, for him. After he hitched the horses to the
carriage he asked me if I wanted a ride. After awhile
I went over on the toboggin slide. I played there a
good while. Then I went in to supper, after supper
drew pictures and then went to bed.

John Tonkins
10 years
Rogers Cottage

After my usual work was done, which consisted of
washing and drying the dishes, I cleaned part of the

Two Hundred Children

pantry, finishing about half past ten, then I helped my cottage mother until half past eleven. As my work then was finished for the morning, I dressed for the afternoon. After dinner I washed and dried the dishes, ironed until half past two, then went out doors with Fanny Smith to take pictures with our camera, returning to the house I read until supper time. After washing and drying the dishes, I went into the parlor and did a little hem-stitching on a handkerchief. About half past eight I went to bed.

Viola Favelet

14 years

Odell Cottage

Last Saturday after breakfast I swept, polished and dusted the third story hall and the stairs. When I had finished this work I dug some worms and went fishing. I stayed all day and returned home with eleven fish which I cleaned and cooked. After cooking my fish I prepared for supper. After supper I worked in the pantry. I scraped the dishes and also helped dry them and put them away. Then I went up stairs, washed, and brushed my teeth. After that I said my prayers and went to bed.

William North

10 years

Graham Cottage

In the morning before breakfast I dressed, washed and combed my hair. After breakfast I made my bed,

The Diary of a Day

swept and flanneled the floor, dusted the chairs and made the room look tidy. Then I went down stairs, dusted the office and flanneled the floor. I also dusted the chairs and tables and helped polish the floor in the parlor. I cleaned the cottage mother's bath room and washed out the basin and bath tub. After that I helped sweep and flannel the hall. After I had finished my work I went down stairs to the basement, washed and combed my hair and went to sewing class. Here I made a skirt for my doll. After dinner I helped upstairs in the attic and when the work there was finished I played for the rest of the afternoon. After supper I went up stairs, read and then went to bed.

Ethel Hammonds
10 years
Odell Cottage

In the morning after breakfast I made my bed and did my usual work. When this was finished I took my bath and then helped in the kitchen until dinner. After dinner I swept the dining room floor and set the table. Then I covered the floor of my rabbit cage with wire so if the rabbits burrowed they could not get out. I put in dirt from two to three inches thick. The afternoon passed so quickly that I had no time to play.

Eugene Gostely
12 years
Rogers Cottage

Before breakfast I molded the bread which I had made the night before. After breakfast, did my usual

Two Hundred Children

Saturday work, which consisted of making my bed, cleaning my cottage mother's bed room and sitting room, and then did my own washing. After which I helped my cottage mother in various ways. After dinner I dressed for sewing class, where I stayed until four o'clock, when I went out and played baseball until supper time. After supper I washed the dishes, did my ironing, studied my Sunday School lesson and then read until bed time.

Alice Allen
15 years
Perkins Cottage

We got up at six o'clock and I did my bathroom work before breakfast. At seven we had our breakfast. After breakfast I did my pantry work and when I had finished it I went outside and raked our road. At eleven o'clock I went fishing with one of the boys, but only caught nine fish. At twelve o'clock I went home for dinner. After dinner I did my pantry work again, and went fishing until four o'clock. We caught a hundred and seventeen Tommy Cods, the largest being over nine inches long and weighing about one half pound. At four o'clock I went to Hastings for the mail. On returning to Bethune I spent the evening reading "Under Drake's Flag."

Verne Jimmerson
15 years
Bethune Cottage

The Diary of a Day

After we had breakfast I did my morning work, which consisted of clearing the dishes off the tables, washing and drying them and then resetting the tables. At nine o'clock I went to sewing class and worked on some underwear until noon. I then came to a good dinner and after we were through I cleared off the tables again and set them for supper. I then went into the library and read a few chapters of "Little Women," which was very interesting. After my eyes got tired of reading, I helped one of the girls pack her grip, preparatory to leaving the Home. We invited two of the girls from Perkins Cottage to spend the afternoon with us, and we had a very pleasant time. After supper I did the dishes again and read more in "Little Women." I also helped two of the younger girls with their lessons.

Mary Dorr
14 years
Hamilton Cottage

After breakfast I did my usual work, which consists of making my bed, scrubbing the basement steps and cleaning the garbage can. Then I got ready and went to the village and got the mail. After it was looked over, I delivered it. At ten o'clock I went to work out in the field, pulling up turnips and rutabagas until noon.

After dinner I helped to clean the store room, and received about a half dozen sweet apples for it. I then played baseball until three o'clock. I saw a wagon going

Two Hundred Children

down the hill and after receiving permission from the driver, some other fellows and I tumbled in the back of the wagon. Landing at the bottom of the hill, we jumped out and had a race down to the bathing houses. I came in last. We fished until supper time and caught about fifty fish, which we cleaned that night and had fried for Sunday morning breakfast. After supper I did my school work for Monday.

Sumner Archer
14 years
Satterlee Cottage

About half past five I awoke and went into the kitchen to prepare breakfast for the girls. The earliest part of the morning was spent in cleaning the kitchen. After dinner I dressed and got ready to take some of the younger girls for a walk. About two o'clock we started and returned home at five. Until supper time I buried my thoughts in the book called, ''The Daughter of an Empress.'' After I had finished my evening work, which is to wash and dry the matron's dishes, I did a little sewing and then prepared my Sunday School lesson for Sunday. We played a few games and then retired.

Ethel Rainbird
16 years
Perkins Cottage

After finishing my usual work, which consisted of scrubbing and cleaning the kitchen, I went fishing. There were quite a number of boys fishing. I caught

The Diary of a Day

ten fish from about one o'clock until half past three. I stopped because when I was throwing out my fishing line one of the hooks caught in my hand and I had a hard time getting it out. I came up home and put a bandage on my hand and went out to play. When the supper bell rang I went into my cottage and helped get supper ready, after which I finished my work and studied some of my lessons.

Charles Goodman

14 years

Graham Cottage

Last Saturday before breakfast I fed my chickens. After breakfast I swept my cottage mother's rooms and the hall. I then helped her with other work until dinner time. After dinner I dried the dishes and set the table. About three o'clock in the afternoon I bought four oranges. I gave two to my brother and kept the rest for myself. About four o'clock I played ball. After playing for awhile I went to supper. After supper I studied my lessons and went to bed.

Louis Maurer

13 years

Satterlee Cottage

I picked dandelions and earned three cents. I played in the afternoon. I polished the hall and I slid down the slide.

Octavius Bruce

8 years

Satterlee Cottage

CHILDREN AND YOUTH
Social Problems and Social Policy

An Arno Press Collection

Abt, Henry Edward. **The Care, Cure and Education of the Crippled Child.** 1924

Addams, Jane. **My Friend, Julia Lathrop.** 1935

American Academy of Pediatrics. **Child Health Services and Pediatric Education:** Report of the Committee for the Study of Child Health Services. 1949

American Association for the Study and Prevention of Infant Mortality. **Transactions of the First Annual Meeting of the American Association for the Study and Prevention of Infant Mortality.** 1910

Baker, S. Josephine. **Fighting For Life.** 1939

Bell, Howard M. **Youth Tell Their Story:** A Study of the Conditions and Attitudes of Young People in Maryland Between the Ages of 16 and 24. 1938

Bossard, James H. S. and Eleanor S. Boll, editors. **Adolescents in Wartime.** 1944

Bossard, James H. S., editor. **Children in a Depression Decade.** 1940

Brunner, Edmund DeS. **Working With Rural Youth.** 1942

Care of Dependent Children in the Late Nineteenth and Early Twentieth Centuries. Introduction by Robert H. Bremner. 1974

Care of Handicapped Children. Introduction by Robert H. Bremner. 1974

[Chenery, William L. and Ella A. Merritt, editors]. **Standards of Child Welfare:** A Report of the Children's Bureau Conferences, May and June, 1919. 1919

The Child Labor Bulletin, 1912, 1913. 1974

Children In Confinement. Introduction by Robert M. Mennel. 1974

Children's Bureau Studies. Introduction by William M. Schmidt. 1974

Clopper, Edward N. **Child Labor in City Streets.** 1912

David, Paul T. **Barriers To Youth Employment.** 1942

Deutsch, Albert. **Our Rejected Children.** 1950

Drucker, Saul and Maurice Beck Hexter. **Children Astray.** 1923

Duffus, R[obert] L[uther] and L. Emmett Holt, Jr. **L. Emmett Holt:** Pioneer of a Children's Century. 1940

Fuller, Raymond G. **Child Labor and the Constitution.** 1923

Holland, Kenneth and Frank Ernest Hill. **Youth in the CCC.** 1942

Jacoby, George Paul. **Catholic Child Care in Nineteenth Century New York:** With a Correlated Summary of Public and Protestant Child Welfare. 1941

Johnson, Palmer O. and Oswald L. Harvey. **The National Youth Administration.** 1938

The Juvenile Court. Introduction by Robert M. Mennel. 1974

Klein, Earl E. **Work Accidents to Minors in Illinois.** 1938

Lane, Francis E. **American Charities and the Child of the Immigrant:** A Study of Typical Child Caring Institutions in New York and Massachusetts Between the Years 1845 and 1880. 1932

The Legal Rights of Children. Introduction by Sanford N. Katz. 1974

Letchworth, William P[ryor]. **Homes of Homeless Children:** A Report on Orphan Asylums and Other Institutions for the Care of Children. [1903]

Lorwin, Lewis. **Youth Work Programs:** Problems and Policies. 1941

Lundberg, Emma O[ctavia] and Katharine F. Lenroot. **Illegitimacy As A Child-Welfare Problem, Parts 1 and 2.** 1920/1921

New York State Commission on Relief for Widowed Mothers. **Report of the New York State Commission on Relief for Widowed Mothers.** 1914

Otey, Elizabeth Lewis. **The Beginnings of Child Labor Legislation in Certain States;** A Comparative Study. 1910

Phillips, Wilbur C. **Adventuring For Democracy.** 1940

Polier, Justine Wise. **Everyone's Children, Nobody's Child:** A Judge Looks At Underprivileged Children in the United States. 1941

Proceedings of the Annual Meeting of the National Child Labor Committee, 1905, 1906. 1974

Rainey, Homer P. **How Fare American Youth?** 1940

Reeder, Rudolph R. **How Two Hundred Children Live and Learn.** 1910

Security and Services For Children. 1974

Sinai, Nathan and Odin W. Anderson. **EMIC (Emergency Maternity and Infant Care):** A Study of Administrative Experience. 1948

Slingerland, W. H. **Child-Placing in Families:** A Manual For Students and Social Workers. 1919

[Solenberger], Edith Reeves. **Care and Education of Crippled Children in the United States.** 1914

Spencer, Anna Garlin and Charles Wesley Birtwell, editors. **The Care of Dependent, Neglected and Wayward Children:** Being a Report of the Second Section of the International Congress of Charities, Correction and Philanthropy, Chicago, June, 1893. 1894

Theis, Sophie Van Senden. **How Foster Children Turn Out.** 1924

Thurston, Henry W. **The Dependent Child:** A Story of Changing Aims and Methods in the Care of Dependent Children. 1930

U.S. Advisory Committee on Education. **Report of the Committee, February, 1938.** 1938

The United States Children's Bureau, 1912-1972. 1974

White House Conference on Child Health and Protection.
Dependent and Neglected Children: Report of the Committee on
Socially Handicapped — Dependency and Neglect. 1933

White House Conference on Child Health and Protection.
**Organization for the Care of Handicapped Children, National,
State, Local.** 1932

White House Conference on Children in a Democracy. **Final Report
of the White House Conference on Children in A Democracy.** [1942]

Wilson, Otto. **Fifty Years' Work With Girls, 1883-1933:** A Story
of the Florence Crittenton Homes. 1933

Wrenn, C. Gilbert and D. L. Harley. **Time On Their Hands:**
A Report on Leisure, Recreation, and Young People. 1941